JAVELIN OVER JERICHO

24 PRINCIPLES OF LEADERSHIP FROM JOSHUA

Nancy Hulshult

Javelin over Jericho: 24 Principles of Leadership From Joshua

ISBN: 979-8-9856988-6-2

Published by:
NarratusCreative | Narratus Press
P.O. Box 1413
Hamilton, OH 45012

Layout/Design: NarratusCreative | narratuscreative.com
Cover Photo Credits: Greg Schanding

Produced in the United States of America

Foreword

For over twenty years, I have had the privilege of leading various organizations in both the private and public sectors. Some of these groups involved only a handful of individuals, while others were comprised of hundreds. Although each group was unique in their size, goals, and missions, they all had one thing in common; they needed someone to lead them.

During my time working in the public education system, I mentored many great leaders and met other individuals who were on their way to becoming great leaders. I watched as school administrators brought forth their best every day to lead their staffs in the mission of educating and improving the lives of the children and families they served. I observed individuals who gave their all to make someone's day just a little bit brighter. I marveled at the resiliency my colleagues demonstrated daily, enduring exceptionally challenging situations and unthinkable obstacles. To these people, I tip my hat and say thank you.

There are few roles that are as challenging as that of being a leader. Leadership requires an immense, balanced skill set that very few individuals actually possess. Throughout history, there have been individuals who have mastered portions of the skill set necessary to be a leader, but rarely has someone been able to master them all.

In my experience, I have found that of all the qualities a leader can possess, the most important is the manner in which leaders treat those they are leading. Followers will forgive mistakes, blunders, even misguidance and misdirection, if they truly believe their leader cares about them and their well-being. Conversely, no matter how strong a leader's other skills are, if their followers don't believe they are cared for, they will cease to follow the leader. Countless organizations fall short of reaching their goals, lose talented members, and drift off course, not because their leader doesn't possess qualities that are agreed upon to be essential for a top-notch leader, rather, they fall short because followers quit supporting the mission because of how they are treated.

For all aspiring leaders who are reading this book, I urge you to never forget that leaders are leaders of people. You must never forget that your existence hinges upon others. If you fail to meet the needs of those that are following you, you will never truly achieve your personal goals or the goals of your organization, business, or entity.

In a world that is in need of strong leaders more than ever before, Dr. Hulshult provides a playbook for leaders to follow from the greatest book on leadership of all time, the Bible. While many best-selling books and military journals have been dedicated to the topic of leadership, few authors have taken the angle of connecting leadership to a prominent individual from the Bible. In Javelin Over Jericho, Dr. Hulshult highlights 24 principles of leadership demonstrated by Joshua. Each of these principles is noteworthy and essential for leaders who want to truly master their craft and meet the needs of their organization and the members involved. I encourage the reader to go through this book multiple times and take advantage of the space provided to write your reflections. These reflections could serve as a crucial tool down the road. Come back to this text, and read your reflections. The recollection of what you were thinking and feeling at the time of reading the text might provide the encouragement you need to overcome the challenges you are facing in your future situation.

In one of my favorite chapters, Dr. Hulshult highlights the power of a leader's words. Although Joshua carried a javelin, his true weapon of choice was his voice. The words he chose (or more accurately, were instilled into him by God) were the true weapon that brought down the walls of Jericho. The words of encouragement provided by Joshua empowered his army to believe they would find victory. They had no doubts that with Jacob's leadership and God's will on their side, they would be victorious, not just at Jericho but over future enemies in the years ahead. With God's will, love and guidance, paired with the principles discussed in this book, your voice can lead your organization to victory as well.

Throughout her years of dedication to local school systems and churches, Dr. Hulshult has earned a place amongst the ranks of great leaders. It is through her dedication and commitment that thousands of people have benefited. I first met Dr. Hulshult when she served in the role of an assistant principal and later worked with her when she was elevated to the status of building principal. Throughout her time working in education, Dr. Hulshult repeatedly demonstrated exceptional qualities of leadership. I can say from first-hand experience that her leadership style and core principles mirrored the principles she shares in this book. I am privileged to say that I worked with her and I am honored to be able to call her a friend.

Whether you are in a position of leadership for the first time in your life, or a long time veteran who wants to challenge yourself to become even better, I encourage you to dive into Javelin Over Jericho with an open mind, ready to take away concepts that will help teach you what it takes to truly be a leader.

Richard Pate, M.Ed.
CEO, Advisor, Coach

Dedication & Appreciation

To Darrell Hulshult, my husband and best friend for life.

To Ben, Mark, and Michael, my sons who teach me far more than I have taught them.

To my grandchildren, Evan, Reese, Madelyn, Andrew, Remy, Alex, Conner, Joey, Seth, Nathan, Bennett, Asher, Aaron, Junie, Noah, who fill my life with love and laughter.

To my spiritual mentors, who keep me grounded in truth, faith, and love:

Pastor Felix R. Escobar

Bishop Michael E. Dantley, Ed.D.

To my faithful friends and editors, who help to correct, clarify, and amplify my thoughts:

Debbie Day

Mary Lou Hudek

Chad P. Shepherd

To Rick Pate, for his encouragement and leadership.

To Denise Chaney, for her ongoing love and support.

Table of Contents

Introduction

"Joshua fought the battle of Jericho, and the walls came tumbling down." Children sing about this famous battle that was fought and won without the use of physical weapons, only spiritual ones: prayer and obedience to God. No other conquest is quite like this.

From high school student council to a degree in administrative and educational leadership, I have studied and lived leadership for most of my life. As I read the Bible in my daily devotions, I tend to focus on the biblical leaders and their characteristics that contributed to their successes and their failures. I love to review their exchanges with God and see how their humility or pride was evident in their growth as leaders. This led me to analyze the unique leadership principles that made Joshua so powerful and successful in his calling from God to establish the Promised Land. Join me in reading and reflecting on the Book of Joshua and how this warrior leader led his people with his javelin and his God.

Front cover of book: This photo is of Nathan Hulshult, one of my grandsons, who sees himself as leader, conqueror, athlete, and winner of all games and conflicts. As a middle child, Nathan has learned to follow his older brother, Seth, and to lead his younger twin brothers, Asher and Aaron. As we were exploring our woods, Nathan chose the biggest walking stick available: the carved eagle head. He insisted on leading us to the creek and then back home again. He teaches me that leadership characteristics are evident very early in life, can be nurtured by more mature leaders, can grow according to opportunities and surroundings, and are most successful when guided by God and Godly people.

When I see Nathan and his eagle staff, I think of Joshua and his javelin. A person doesn't necessarily need to use his weapon of choice, if he knows how to lead. We teach Nathan to choose his words rather than weapons to resolve conflicts. In Joshua, we see that he also used words over weapons in the battle of Jericho, and with God as his leader, "the walls came tumbling down."

Back cover photo: the wilderness near Mount Baker, Washington, taken by my good friend and nature photographer, Greg Schanding.

CHAPTER ONE

GREAT LEADERS ARE EQUIPPED AND EXPERIENCED

Summary:

Verses 1-2: After the death of Moses the servant of the Lord, the Lord said to Joshua son of Nun, Moses' aide: 2 "Moses my servant is dead. Now then, you and all these people, get ready to cross the Jordan River into the land I am about to give to them—to the Israelites."

Joshua had been an obedient and trustworthy aide, serving as Moses' military leader, scout, and spiritual mentee. Joshua and Caleb were the only two scouts who brought back good news to Moses about the Promised Land, saying that it could be conquered. They had gone against the bad reports of the other 10 scouts who said, "The Land we explored devours those living in it. All the people we saw there are of great size." Numbers 13:32 Because of their trust in God and steadfast obedience, Joshua and Caleb were the only two people to enter the Promised Land. The rest of the people had shown disobedience and died in the wilderness. After witnessing the death of all but one sojourner who had traveled from Egypt through the desert, including the death of his lifelong mentor Moses, Joshua was now called by God to prepare the descendents and the new generation of Israelites to cross the Jordan River into the Promised Land.

Imagine the mixed emotions of Joshua in this moment: grief from the loss of his longtime mentor and all of his elders who were alive since Egypt; awe of hearing from God; humility of being called by God as leader of his people; relief to know that the 40-year journey was over; elation that he and his people would finally enter the Promised Land; perhaps anxiety about crossing the river with all the people and their possessions; and certainly anticipation of the upcoming battles to conquer the land of the giant-sized people, as described by his scouting colleagues.

For Joshua, this defining moment of leadership called for complete obedience to God. Not only was Joshua described by God as "a man in whom is the spirit of leadership" (Numbers 27:18), Joshua had also learned the best and worst leadership lessons from Moses. Simply put, obedience to God = long life; disobedience to God = death. God had already placed the spirit of leadership in Joshua, originally named Hoshea ("salvation" in Hebrew) then renamed by Moses as Yehoshua ("YHWH God is deliverance").

God chose just the right leaders for his purposes. Consider Moses. To oppose the great Pharaoh of Egypt, God called Moses, a man with a speech defect who questioned God on a regular basis. Consider the juxtaposition of Pharaoh with Moses. Pharaoh was a wealthy leader, who was considered a god and had the power of position, symbolized by his golden scepter, as well as the power of his magicians. Moses was a defector of the palace turned shepherd, who held the lowest position of power, symbolized by wooden staff and a sidekick brother to speak for him. All odds would be in Pharaoh's favor, were it not for the Almighty God, powerful in words and deeds to show his authority over all of the land and its people. All honor and glory would be the Lord's, not any man's.

Consider Aaron, who obeyed his calling to assist his brother Moses through the Exodus from Egypt. His speaking abilities and his ability to follow were perfect for God's purposes in assisting Moses. However, left on his own at the foot of the mountain, Aaron failed as a leader of the people, who pressured him into crafting a golden idol for them to worship while Moses was meeting with God on the mountain. They lost patience with Moses, faith in God, and trust in Aaron to lead. He became a goldsmith and leader in idolatry.

The next leader to be called by God is Joshua to replace Moses. Joshua was on the mountain while Moses was receiving the commandments from God. Meanwhile, Aaron and the people were at the foot of the mountain worshiping the golden calf.

"When Joshua heard the noise of the people shouting, he said to Moses, 'There is the sound of war in the camp.'" —Exodus 32:17

This confirms that Joshua was not involved in the idolatry. He was with Moses going up the mountain, going to the tent of meeting, and accompanying Moses to most places where Moses exercised his leadership. Joshua was a good follower as well as a good leader. He was a great scout with great faith in God, and he was a dutiful assistant to Moses. Joshua did not inherit his leadership position. He was not the son but the mentee of Moses, called, prepared, and poised for leadership. Along with Moses, Joshua had participated in the first Passover, the parting of the Red Sea, the desert manna and quail provisions, and the battle over the Amalekites while Moses raised his arms. He was a faithful follower, a strong warrior, and a witness to God's glory present in the tabernacle, where he remained even as Moses returned to camp in Exodus 33. Joshua watched at the door of the tent of meeting as Moses went into the presence of God and spoke to the Lord face to face, but when Moses left, Joshua stayed. Apparently, he wanted more of the glory of God.

> Now Moses used to take a tent and pitch it outside the camp some distance away, calling it the "tent of meeting." Anyone inquiring of the Lord would go to the tent of meeting outside the camp. 8 And whenever Moses went out to the tent, all the people rose and stood at the entrances to their tents, watching Moses until he entered the tent. 9 As Moses went into the tent, the pillar of cloud would come down and stay at the entrance, while the Lord spoke with Moses. 10 Whenever the people saw the pillar of cloud standing at the entrance to the tent, they all stood and worshiped, each at the entrance to their tent. 11 The Lord would speak to Moses face to face, as one speaks to a friend. Then Moses would return to the camp, but his young aide Joshua son of Nun did not leave the tent. —Exodus 33:7-11

> Verse 3: I will give you every place where you set your foot, as I promised Moses. 4 Your territory will extend from the desert to Lebanon, and from the great river, the Euphrates—all the Hittite country—to the Mediterranean Sea in the west.

God's promise to Moses was sent on through Joshua. Yes, every piece of land where Joshua set his foot would belong to him and his people. This must have been as overwhelming as God's promise to Abraham that his descendants would be as "numerous as the stars" (Genesis 22:17). Of course, the catch was that the Israelites would have to conquer the people inhabiting that land. However, God accompanied his promises with his continual presence and support, as in verse 5.

Verse 5: No one will be able to stand against you all the days of your life. As I was with Moses, so I will be with you; I will never leave you nor forsake you.

For the times when we are called by God to lead, to follow, to conquer, to endure, to do something new or unfamiliar, and to take courageous action, we can remember that God will be by our side to accomplish the specific purposes for which he has called us.

Verse 6: Be strong and courageous, because you will lead these people to inherit the land I swore to their ancestors to give them.

Verse 7: "Be strong and very courageous. Be careful to obey all the law my servant Moses gave you; do not turn from it to the right or to the left, that you may be successful wherever you go.

Verse 8: Keep this Book of the Law always on your lips; meditate on it day and night, so that you may be careful to do everything written in it. Then you will be prosperous and successful.

Verse 9: Have I not commanded you? Be strong and courageous. Do not be afraid; do not be discouraged, for the Lord your God will be with you wherever you go."

For the third time, God tells Joshua to be strong and courageous. There is no doubt of God's purpose in emphasizing these words and the reality that Joshua surely would hear them and would need to remember them as he faces all the conquests and challenges ahead.

God's formula for success for Joshua in this chapter:

1. Be strong and courageous - qualities necessary and available to anyone who wants to follow God. These are traits that can be developed and exercised with practice.

2. Obey all Moses' instructions - specific rules and procedures that were passed through the generations, some written in stone, and some learned through oral tradition. These take study and practice to be able to remember and to pass on to the next generation.

3. Do not deviate - This is a warning to stay focused on God only. Any turning to the left or the right can get us off course from God and his purposes. "Don't even (think about it)...!"

4. Meditate day and night on the Book of Instructions - this describes planned and routine time with God and God's word. To meditate is to think deeply, to analyze, to ponder, to spend extended time in understanding God at a deeper level.

5. Do not be afraid or discouraged - The words "afraid" and "discouraged" are antithetical to the words "strong and courageous." To be weak is to be afraid. To be disheartened is to lack courage and strength of heart. God delivered this message to Joshua in positive and negative contexts.

God's promises to Joshua:

1. Joshua would enter and conquer the Promised Land with his people.

2. God's presence would be with Joshua wherever he went.

Verses 10-11: 10 So Joshua ordered the officers of the people: 11 "Go through the camp and tell the people, 'Get your provisions ready. Three days from now you will cross the Jordan here to go in and take possession of the land the Lord your God is giving you for your own.'"

The Israelites were used to traveling on the fly, going and staying depending on the cloud by day and the fire by night. In this case, they were given three days, certainly significant in retrospect, given the three days from Jesus' death to resurrection. Going from the wilderness to the Promised Land was to take place in three days. On the other hand, they were given three days to prepare all their possessions for crossing a river, a feat of its own, even if it were on dry ground. Did they know that God would make a way for them to cross on dry land? They would have known the story of the parting of the Red Sea, and this was just a river. Even when the waters parted and the Ark of the Covenant would be held by the priests in the middle of the Jordan, "the people hurried", according to Joshua 4:10. It reminds me of mission trips when we say, "Hurry up and wait." We always need to be ready to move, even when there are times of waiting or when plans change. When God says to move, we move! We can take that lesson from the Israelites.

> Verses 12-15: 12 But to the Reubenites, the Gadites and the half-tribe of Manasseh, Joshua said, 13 "Remember the command that Moses the servant of the Lord gave you after he said, 'The Lord your God will give you rest by giving you this land.' 14 Your wives, your children and your livestock may stay in the land that Moses gave you east of the Jordan, but all your fighting men, ready for battle, must cross over ahead of your fellow Israelites. You are to help them 15 until the Lord gives them rest, as he has done for you, and until they too have taken possession of the land the Lord your God is giving them. After that, you may go back and occupy your own land, which Moses the servant of the Lord gave you east of the Jordan toward the sunrise."

We're all in this together, according to God. Not only did God promise to be with Joshua, he commanded the families staying on the east side of Jordan to help the west siders by sending their men to battle for the land on the west side. 4:13 says that 40,000 men, armed and ready for battle, crossed the Jordan. Joshua's army was well equipped, according to God's promise.

Verse 16: Then they answered Joshua, "Whatever you have commanded us we will do, and wherever you send us we will go.

The followers of Joshua had learned to readily accept the commands by God as given to him. At least at this point in history, the new generations crossing over the Jordan to the Promised Land are learning to obey wholeheartedly, without complaining, doubting, or rebelling. May we today learn to say, *"Whatever you have commanded, we will do, and wherever you send us, we will go."*

Reflection:

1. What time has come for me to "get ready" or "to cross" in leadership? In ministry?

2. What is the territory of influence that God has mapped out for me?

3. Is there any person or thing that is standing against me that requires me to have faith that God is with me always? Knowing that God is with me, what must I do to be an overcomer?

4. What causes me to be strong and courageous? How have I been strong and courageous in the past that has brought me success in the eyes of God?

5. Have I deviated from God's Word? If I have, how do I right my course?

6. Do I meditate on God's Word every day and night? How does my meditation and prayer time affect my daily life?

7. Have I committed my life to God by promising, "Whatever you have commanded, I will do, and wherever you send me, I will go"?

LEADERSHIP TIP #1: GREAT LEADERS ARE EQUIPPED AND EXPERIENCED.

The difference in Moses' and Joshua's calling into leadership was that God called Moses after he had failed and before he proved himself trustworthy. Joshua proved himself before he was put in a leadership position.

"That's a good example of how leaders should be chosen. The failure in leadership in churches and in the world happens when potential leaders are not made to prove themselves before they are handed leadership positions." — Debbie Day

Response:

_____

_____

_____

_____

_____

_____

_____

_____

_____

_____

_____

_____

_____

_____

_____

CHAPTER TWO

GREAT LEADERS
PLAN STRATEGIES

Summary:

Verse 1: Then Joshua son of Nun secretly sent two spies from Shittim. "Go, look over the land," he said, "especially Jericho." So they went and entered the house of a prostitute named Rahab and stayed there.

Once a spy himself, Joshua sent two spies to check out Jericho, the first city that he planned to conquer. Moses had sent 12 spies, and only Joshua and Caleb brought back a good report. Joshua decided to send just two spies, which speaks of the level of trust in them. They went to the most likely and unlikely place for information and safety: the house of a prostitute. What made it the most likely? It was a place commonly known to be an exchange of public information whispered within hidden walls that shadowed both native and foreign citizens. Information flowed like the money that exchanged countless hands. The spies were strategic in keeping their identity private while finding a safe place to rest. Most unlikely was the participation or distraction of the spies in the practice of prostitution, undoubtedly chosen by Joshua for their godliness, loyalty, trust, wisdom, and obedience. The conquest of the Promised Land hinged on the valuable information brought back to Joshua by these two men. The prostitute Rahab had already heard of the Israelites and was ready to protect them in exchange for her and her family's protection. Ironically, in this house of prostitution, the spies and Rahab exchanged something more valuable than either money or sex: their very lives! Not only did they have to trust each other, they also had to trust God in this most unlikely relationship. From this, God's purpose for his people was being fulfilled.

Consider another moment in the Bible when God brought together the most unlikely people in a supernatural exchange that served God's purposes. As Peter and John walked past the temple gates, they passed a member of the "undesirables" of society: a beggar, lame from birth. The beggar called out for money from them but could not look them in the eyes because of his status or his feeling of being unworthy. In Acts 3:4, *Peter said to him, "Look at us!" Then Peter said, "Silver or gold I do not have, but what I do have I give you. In the name of Jesus Christ of Nazareth, walk."* (Acts 3:5)

Instead of an exchange of money, they exchanged trust in God and each other for the lame man's healing. Like Rahab, the lame man found something more valuable than money: his life through the power of healing in Jesus' name. The lame man had to make the attempt to get up and walk, and he did! Then as he held on to the apostles, they became the center of attention as God's purpose for his people was being fulfilled. After disowning Jesus Christ, their Messiah, the people flocked to Peter, who was able to offer the Israelites faith and new life in that same Jesus:

> *While the man held on to Peter and John, all the people were astonished and came running to them in the place called Solomon's Colonnade. 12 When Peter saw this, he said to them: "Fellow Israelites, why does this surprise you? Why do you stare at us as if by our own power or godliness we had made this man walk? 13 The God of Abraham, Isaac and Jacob, the God of our fathers, has glorified his servant Jesus. You handed him over to be killed, and you disowned him before Pilate, though he had decided to let him go. 14 You disowned the Holy and Righteous One and asked that a murderer be released to you. 15 You killed the author of life, but God raised him from the dead. We are witnesses of this. 16 By faith in the name of Jesus, this man whom you see and know was made strong. It is Jesus' name and the faith that comes through him that has completely healed him, as you can all see. — Acts 3:11-16*

With examples like these, we can be aware of the most unlikely circumstances that bring people together from different walks of life to advance God's purposes for his people.

Verse 6: (But she had taken them up to the roof and hidden them under the stalks of flax she had laid out on the roof.)

Imagine what the spies might have thought as they lay hidden under flax on the roof of a prostitute's house. Anyone without previous knowledge of these men might have thought that they were guilty customers hiding in anonymity and shame. Sometimes the most godly missions put people in situations that may seem otherwise to the casual observer: sharing a meal with a homeless person, witnessing to people in a bar, taking a single pregnant woman to the doctor, visiting a prisoner, and other times when godly people minister to people in different walks of life.

> *Verses 8-9: Before the spies lay down for the night, she went up on the roof 9 and said to them, "I know that the Lord has given you this land and that a great fear of you has fallen on us, so that all who live in this country are melting in fear because of you.*

Rahab visited the men as they lay down for the night. Instead of the usual nightly event for a prostitute, this visit from Rahab showed the spies what was in her mind, her soul, and her heart. First, she showed them what she knew in her mind about the Red Sea deliverance and the conquests over the two kings.

> *Verse 10: We have heard how the Lord dried up the water of the Red Sea for you when you came out of Egypt, and what you did to Sihon and Og, the two kings of the Amorites east of the Jordan, whom you completely destroyed.*

> *Verse 11: When we heard of it, our hearts melted in fear and everyone's courage failed because of you, for the Lord your God is God in heaven above and on the earth below.*

Secondly, Rahab acknowledged from her soul that the Lord their God is God of heaven and earth. From her soul, she knows that God is all powerful and ruler of heaven and earth.

> *Verse 12-13: 12 "Now then, please swear to me by the Lord that you will show kindness to my family, because I have shown kindness to you. Give me a sure sign 13 that you will spare the lives of my father and mother, my brothers and sisters, and all who belong to them—and that you will save us from death."*

Thirdly, Rahab showed the spies what was in her heart. She wanted them to spare her life and the life of her family. Not only did she want their kindness in return for the kindness shown to them, Rahab wanted them to swear to her by the Lord. This gesture is a bond of trust and faith among them.

Here Rahab and her family are grafted into the salvation story. Forever they have guaranteed protection with the people of Israel, God's people. Rahab is included in the genealogy of Jesus, which shows how God honors our obedience in spite of our weaknesses.

"Consider the 'scandalous' characters in the lineage of Jesus: Isaac wasn't Abraham's first son (scandal); Tamar's husband dies, his brother can't fulfill his obligation and is killed by God, so then she dresses like a prostitute and seduces her father-in-law (scandal on scandal on scandal); then we have this story of Rahab (scandal); and then Boaz who marries Ruth (powerful story); of course, the scandals of King David; and finally, even Jesus himself is born into scandal as everyone knows that Joseph is NOT his father... and you know how small towns talk! In every one of these stories of scandal, there is also REDEMPTION. Even in the lineage of Jesus and his very birth... it is REDEMPTION, REDEMPTION, REDEMPTION!!!" – Chad P. Shepherd

Verse 17-18: 17 Now the men had said to her, "This oath you made us swear will not be binding on us 18 unless, when we enter the land, you have tied this scarlet cord in the window through which you let us down, and unless you have brought your father and mother, your brothers and all your family into your house.

Rahab's deliverance came with further action from her and her family: to tie her scarlet cord in her window and to have the whole family gather together in her house. As we imagine the spies hiding in the flax, imagine also Rahab's family gathering in a house of prostitution for the sake of saving all their lives. Everyone had to trust each other and the purposes of God.

Verse 22: When they left, they went into the hills and stayed there three days, until the pursuers had searched all along the road and returned without finding them.

What's more dangerous or more uncomfortable? Hiding in the house of a prostitute or hiding in the hills for three days while the spies were being pursued? Through their reconnaissance mission, the spies showed courage, wisdom, and perseverance. Joshua chose wisely.

Reflection:

1. What unlikely people in my life have crossed my path and have shown me more about the love and faith in Jesus Christ?

2. When have I been in a dangerous or precarious position in my life that caused me to trust in others while I trusted in God?

3. When have others acknowledged the power of God and the fear of God, even when they didn't believe in God themselves? How did I use that acknowledgment to guide them further into a mind, soul, and heart knowledge of God?

4. Who is grafted into my family, into my family of God, because of God's intervention and plan of salvation?

5. The scarlet rope is a visible sign of deliverance in the story of Rahab and the spies. What is a visible sign or symbol of deliverance for me? For my family? Others in my life?

LEADERSHIP TIP #2: GREAT LEADERS PLAN STRATEGIES

Great leaders use strategic planning, including gathering facts, talking to knowledgeable people of integrity, consulting with other people (more than just one person), assessing data, evaluating evidence, and deciding when to take action. Both Moses and Joshua used similar strategies when sending spies to the Promised Land to see what the greatest challenges were going to be in order to conquer the land. For both leaders, they were successful. When Joshua and Caleb were spies for Moses, they were the only two of the twelve spies that had opposing opinions, but Moses trusted them as having the most accurate assessment of the situation. Joshua, perhaps because of his experience himself spying for Moses, only sent two trusted spies, who were able to make an ally in the person of the prostitute Rahab. Great leaders utilize trustworthy followers to network with other people valuable to their mission. Effective leaders have trusted friends and influence inside and outside of their camp.

As you read through the book of Joshua, watch for elements of his strategic planning. Does he demonstrate good strategic planning throughout his time as leader of Israel? You can remember some basic principles with the following acronym: C-SALT[1].

Response:

_____

_____

_____

_____

_____

_____

_____

_____

_____

---

[1]King (see King, Bonds-Raacke, & Saylor, 2011) lists five C-SALT principles for successful strategic planning: Collaboration, Specificity, Assessment, Leadership, and Transparency. https://www.uncp.edu/resources/institutional-research/key-resources-links/strategic-planning/guiding-principles#:~:text=She%20identifies%20these%20as%20the,for%20achieving%20an%20organization's%20vision.

CHAPTER THREE

GREAT LEADERS TRUST AND ARE TRUSTWORTHY

Summary:

Verse 1: Early in the morning Joshua and all the Israelites set out from Shittim and went to the Jordan, where they camped before crossing over.

Once a spy himself, Joshua sent two spies to check out Jericho, theThis move of the Israelites had to be a journey of faith as they camped by the Jordan River flowing with no dry land over which to cross. Imagine what they must have been thinking about their leader's decision, about God, about their future. They could actually see their Promised Land just on the other side of the river! Imagine how their prayers must have sounded during their time of waiting. Was their faith stronger because of their Red Sea deliverance?

Verse 2-4: 2 After three days the officers went throughout the camp, 3 giving orders to the people: "When you see the ark of the covenant of the Lord your God, and the Levitical priests carrying it, you are to move out from your positions and follow it. 4 Then you will know which way to go, since you have never been this way before. But keep a distance of about two thousand cubits between you and the ark; do not go near it."

Not only did the Israelites have to follow Joshua's and the officers' orders, they also had to follow the tribe(s) in front of them as they moved out toward the place of crossing. None of them had ever been this way before, so they were dependent on others to lead them and had to trust that their leaders had heard God clearly and correctly.

Verse 5: Joshua told the people, "Consecrate yourselves, for tomorrow the Lord will do amazing things among you."

God is a pure being and humans can experience his holiness in pure spaces. As God was preparing to work a miracle in their lives, the people were preparing their hearts, souls, minds, and bodies to receive the miracle in its completeness.

Verse 7:And the Lord said to Joshua, "Today I will begin to exalt you in the eyes of all Israel, so they may know that I am with you as I was with Moses.

Leadership is a process. This day was to be the beginning of the type of respect shown for Joshua like that shown for Moses, and this day was to be confirmation that God was with Joshua as with Moses. This defining moment was God's affirmation of Joshua's leadership and God's confirmation of his faithfulness to be with Joshua as he was with Moses.

Verse 8: Tell the priests who carry the ark of the covenant: 'When you reach the edge of the Jordan's waters, go and stand in the river.'"

The priests were asked to walk into a river at flood stage (see verse 15) together while carrying a load with two stone tablets before any water had stopped flowing. Not only did they have to keep their own footing, they also had to protect and balance their load. What if they lost their balance or grip, and they or the ark of the covenant went floating down the river? What a responsibility for these priests to take steps of faith into a flowing river where they had not been before with no idea of what was to happen next! Even holy priests set apart for God's service must have had their faith challenged at the banks of the river. Their intellects might have warned them of their precarious positions, but their faith would override logic, at least logic of the human kind. What sometimes appears to be illogical or unnatural to people is often logical in God's plan to do the miraculous and supernatural. It can be a test of our faith. If everything were logical and easy, we would not have to trust God.

Verses 9-13: 9 Joshua said to the Israelites, "Come here and listen to the words of the Lord your God. 10 This is how you will know that the living God is among you and that he will certainly drive out before you the Canaanites, Hittites, Hivites, Perizzites, Girgashites, Amorites and Jebusites. 11 See, the ark of the covenant of the Lord of all the earth will go into the Jordan ahead of you. 12 Now then, choose twelve men from the tribes of Israel, one from each tribe. 13 And as soon as the priests who carry the ark of the Lord— the Lord of all the earth—set foot in the Jordan, its waters flowing downstream will be cut off and stand up in a heap."This is how you will know that the living God is among you and that he will certainly drive out before you the Canaanites, Hittites, Hivites, Perizzites, Girgashites, Amorites and Jebusites.

In Godly leadership, Joshua called the people together to listen to the words of God. He told them that their living God was among them and would go ahead of them to drive out the inhabitants of their Promised Land. To bolster their faith and to prove his intentions of this, God said that he would also go ahead of them–literally–into the Jordan River in the form of the Ark of the Covenant. The priests, not the warriors, led the way carrying God's commandments. By this demonstration, the people would know and God would be faithful to his covenant with them.

Verse 15: Now the Jordan is at flood stage all during harvest. Yet as soon as the priests who carried the ark reached the Jordan and their feet touched the water's edge, 16 the water from upstream stopped flowing. It piled up in a heap a great distance away, at a town called Adam in the vicinity of Zarethan, while the water flowing down to the Sea of the Arabah (that is, the Dead Sea) was completely cut off. So the people crossed over opposite Jericho.

God's miracles are spectacular and undeniable. Since the Jordan River was at flood stage all during harvest, we see that God set the stage for the miracle. Since the waters stopped upstream and downstream as soon as the priests' feet touched the water, we see that God's timing was perfect for the miracle. Since the people crossed over opposite Jericho, the city of their first conquest, we see that God's setting was perfect for the miracle. God had set everything in motion to prove to the people that their covenant together would continue into the Promised Land. Miracles happen because of faith, and faith happens because of miracles.

Verse 17: The priests who carried the ark of the covenant of the Lord stopped in the middle of the Jordan and stood on dry ground, while all Israel passed by until the whole nation had completed the crossing on dry ground.

This scene had to have been poignant for the people as they were in the midst of crossing a body of water on dry ground, similar to their deliverance from the Egyptians at the crossing of the Red Sea, except this time they passed by priests holding the visible sacred sign of God's covenant with them–right in the middle of the river–right in the middle of their deliverance–right in the middle of their miracle!

The Red Sea deliverance was from their captivity in Egypt; the second was from the wilderness and all things of their past: their Egyptian captors, their deceased relatives who worshiped the golden calf, even their repetitive meals of food from heaven. They were starting with a "clean slate" as they were being washed in the Jordan waters, the same waters where Jesus would be baptized by John at the start of Jesus' public ministry. The people had been ceremonially purified and now physically cleansed as they crossed safely on dry land in the middle of a flooded river during harvest. Surely this was their greatest season of harvest: they were moving toward the opposite bank of the river toward Jericho to reap the harvest of land provided by God for them. Jericho would be the first of many conquests on dry land with God leading them all the way!

Reflection:

1. The verses Joshua 1:11, 2:16, 3:2, and 9:16 make references to three days. There are also references to three days or the third day in Genesis, Exodus, and many other books of the bible. Before Jesus rose from the dead on the third day, what would the Israelites have understood about the significance of three days? Would they have understood that three days was part of God's covenant and new life language? Search for "three days" or "third day" on your Bible app and watch the pattern emerge.

2. The Ark of the Covenant holding the Ten Commandments by God led the Israelites across the Jordan River. How do I live my life following the Word of God daily?

3. Do I consider myself purified for God? If not, what do I need to do to be purified in order to do greater wonders in my spiritual life?

4. In my leadership roles in my family, church, job, mission, or circle of friends, what first steps do I need to take to be a better leader for God and his people?

5. For the priests carrying the Ark of the Covenant, they had to take the first few steps into the river before the waters receded. What are my next first steps of faith for me that God is waiting for me to take before moving in my life?

6. One person from each of the twelve tribes of Israel were chosen. In the next chapter, we read that they were to carry a stone from the middle of the Jordan River where the priests stood with the Ark of the Covenant. Joshua had the stones placed together for the people to remember the miracle that God had done for them. Who are the "tribal leaders" in my life? What memorials exist today that represent my "tribe", our faith, and how God has delivered us?

7. Verse 17 says that the whole nation had completed the crossing on dry ground. What would have to happen for our whole nation to be delivered by God?

LEADERSHIP TIP #3: GREAT LEADERS TRUST AND ARE TRUSTWORTHY.

Great leaders can be trusted and know whom to trust. Notwithstanding that God is the consummate leader who can be trusted and knows whom to trust, Joshua also trusted the Levite priests carrying the Ark of the Covenant to step into the flooded waters of the Jordan River before being able to walk across on dry ground. The priests had to trust Joshua, who had to trust God. Because of the level of trust among all these leaders, a miracle happened, and the mission was accomplished.

Response:

_____

_____

_____

_____

_____

_____

_____

_____

_____

_____

_____

_____

CHAPTER FOUR

GREAT LEADERS RECOGNIZE AND CELEBRATE SUCCESS

Summary:

Verse 1-3: When the whole nation had finished crossing the Jordan, the Lord said to Joshua, 2 "Choose twelve men from among the people, one from each tribe, 3 and tell them to take up twelve stones from the middle of the Jordan, from right where the priests are standing, and carry them over with you and put them down at the place where you stay tonight."

Imagine what the people might have been thinking as they rested for their first night on the west side of the Jordan River in the land promised to them for generations. Imagine looking at the stone from your tribe that had been carried from the middle of the river and then looking at the flooding waters of the Jordan that flowed swiftly over the place where your entire nation had just traveled. People can be so quick to forget what God has done for them, or they distort the truth and morph the details. Apparently God wanted to ensure that what they had just experienced was real, supernatural, and worthy of remembering and retelling for future generations, making sure to give God the glory. If they forgot the meaning of the Jordan riverbed stones, they could always refer to the stone tablets in the Ark of the Covenant, namely commandment number one:

Verses 4-8: 4 So Joshua called together the twelve men he had appointed from the Israelites, one from each tribe, 5 and said to them, "Go over before the ark of the Lord your God into the middle of the Jordan. Each of you is to take up a stone on his shoulder, according to the number of the tribes of the Israelites, 6 to serve as a sign among you. In the future, when your children ask you, 'What do these stones mean?' 7 tell them that the flow of the Jordan was cut off before the ark of the covenant of the Lord. When it crossed the Jordan, the waters of the Jordan were cut off. These stones are to be a memorial to the people of Israel forever."

Each stone carrier that represented each of the twelve tribes of Israel was not identified by name nor by criteria. Did each tribe choose the strongest (to carry a stone on his shoulder), the best swimmer (just in case), the most spiritual, the most courageous? Scripture does not delineate names nor attributes of the stone carriers, but they were important participants in the corporate memory and storytelling of God's deliverance and miraculous wonders for future generations. Perhaps their stories had special details about the task, their particular stone, the weight of it as it was carried to shore, and the significance of it stacked with the eleven other stones to commemorate this event in the history of Israel, of God's people. The anonymous participants in the salvation story are just as fascinating as those whose names we know and remember, perhaps because it is easier to see ourselves in their position instead of a known hero or heroine.

Verse 9: Joshua set up the twelve stones that had been in the middle of the Jordan at the spot where the priests who carried the ark of the covenant had stood. And they are there to this day.

Still in existence today, according to scripture, are twelve stones placed together; twelve large stones heavy enough to be carried on a man's shoulder; twelve uncut stones in an unnatural setting as they were taken from the bottom of a river and placed a good distance away on dry ground.

Verses 10-11: 10 Now the priests who carried the ark remained standing in the middle of the Jordan until everything the Lord had commanded Joshua was done by the people, just as Moses had directed Joshua. The people hurried over, 11 and as soon as all of them had crossed, the ark of the Lord and the priests came to the other side while the people watched.

These verses describe several significant details:

1. Joshua is paralleled with Moses in this crossing on dry land; drawing the comparison of miraculous deliverances and comparison of leadership;

2. The people hurried over, which prompts the question of why they felt the need to hurry - lack of trust, anticipation for

the Promised Land, conscious of the amount of daylight left?;

3. Tthe ark and the priests cross last, which means God and his Ark of the Covenant both started and completed this miracle. With faith, the priests stepped in, as the Lord commanded, and with faith, they stayed until all had crossed, as the Lord commanded. All miracles start and end with the glory of God.

4. All the people watched as the Ark of the Covenant was carried safely to shore by the priests, set aside to care for the temple of God. This must have been an impressive scene: ALL the people saved and watching the priests carrying this tangible sign of God's commandments and God's covenant, as if to demonstrate, "I promised, and I have delivered you to this land." God will always have the first and last word in the history of his creation.

Verse 18: And the priests came up out of the river carrying the ark of the covenant of the Lord. No sooner had they set their feet on the dry ground than the waters of the Jordan returned to their place and ran at flood stage as before.

Lest the people and we forget, this story started with a river that was flooding, no small task to cross...unless you are God with power over all creation. Watching the waters return to that level must have been impressive, perhaps the splash of the waters smacking together from upstream and downstream, or simply the rush of the waters from upstream. Regardless of how it happened, who could not resist staring at the place in the river where a whole nation of people had just traveled?

Verse 20: And Joshua set up at Gilgal the twelve stones they had taken out of the Jordan.

East of Jericho at Gilgal ("circle of stones" in Hebrew) are the twelve stones taken out of the Jordan that are still there "to this day". Whether they are covered by layers of earth, eroded by winds, or stuck in the mud (or whether they were destroyed because Gilgal became a place of idol worship later in Israel's history under the judges), archeologists will have to discern.

> *Verses 21-24: 21 He (Joshua) said to the Israelites, "In the future when your descendants ask their parents, 'What do these stones mean?' 22 tell them, 'Israel crossed the Jordan on dry ground.' 23 For the Lord your God dried up the Jordan before you until you had crossed over. The Lord your God did to the Jordan what he had done to the Red Sea when he dried it up before us until we had crossed over. 24 He did this so that all the peoples of the earth might know that the hand of the Lord is powerful and so that you might always fear the Lord your God."*

Joshua is an exemplary leader as he models for the people what they are to tell their descendants about the crossing of the Jordan River on dry land. Just as they had been retelling the story of the Red Sea, they were to retell this story of God's power. Joshua reminded them that God works wonders so that ALL people might know of him and his power. Joshua adds that this event is motivation for them to always fear the Lord. After all, they were witnesses and recipients of his power over nature and his ability to lead them to the Promised Land. Surely they had also remembered or witnessed God's power when he was disobeyed. They didn't know that they were soon going to be asked to conquer Jericho merely with horn blasts and shouting.

Reflection:

1. What is my story of God's providence to tell my children and grandchildren? Do I have a memorial for God's miracles in my life?

2. Why did the people hurry across the dry land in the middle of the Jordan River? Did they not trust that the miracle would sustain them all? Have I ever rushed or hurried through a miracle or movement of God? Are there times when I should stay calm and enjoy the supernatural working of God, even when natural circumstances would otherwise cause me to rush?

3. What is the significance of the piles of stones as memorials to God's powerful miracles in the lives of the Israelites? Compared to the Pyramids of Egypt, the totem poles of Native Americans, the Taj Mahal of India, or the Moai statues of Easter Island, what makes God's rock memorials so distinctive for the Israelites? For us today?

4. If I were charged to represent my tribe and carry a stone from the middle of the Jordan where the priests had stood, what type, size, and shape of stone might I have chosen? Why?

5. How many anonymous people can I recall from the Old and New Testament? How does their anonymity add to the purpose of their stories?

LEADERSHIP TIP #4: GREAT LEADERS RECOGNIZE AND CELEBRATE SUCCESS.

Great leaders recognize and celebrate people when they are successful. God told Joshua to choose twelve people, one from each tribe, to carry a stone from the middle of the river to make a memorial. By doing this, Joshua recognized each tribe, and collaboratively, they created a marker to remember the miracle and the successful safe crossing into the Promised Land.

In 1 Corinthians, chapter 12, Paul describes the importance of having unity and diversity in one body:

12 Just as a body, though one, has many parts, but all its many parts form one body, so it is with Christ. 13 For we were all baptized by one Spirit so as to form one body—whether Jews or Gentiles, slave or free—and we were all given the one Spirit to drink. 14 Even so the body is not made up of one part but of many.

Response:

_____

_____

_____

_____

_____

_____

_____

_____

_____

_____

_____

_____

_____

CHAPTER FIVE

GREAT LEADERS COMMAND UNITY AND DEMAND LOYALTY

Summary:

Verse 1: Now when all the Amorite kings west of the Jordan and all the Canaanite kings along the coast heard how the Lord had dried up the Jordan before the Israelites until they had crossed over, their hearts melted in fear and they no longer had the courage to face the Israelites.

God fought the Israelites' battles for them by the miracle of drying up the Jordan River for them to cross. Before ever seeing or meeting the Israelites, the kings were in terror and lost their courage to face them. God still fights Christians' battles with powerful miracles today, but somehow non-Christian leaders aren't melting in fear. Perhaps non-Christians are not hearing of God's power in our lives, or perhaps Christians are not testifying to the world about God's miraculous power and sovereignty. Christians are being persecuted in countries around the world, and many people, Christians and non-Christians alike, don't even know or don't seem to care enough to help fight for their lives.

"It's like the magicians of Pharaoh; there are so many counterfeit miracles on the web, it's hard to believe any." — Debbie Day

Verses 2-3: 2 At that time the Lord said to Joshua, "Make flint knives and circumcise the Israelites again." 3 So Joshua made flint knives and circumcised the Israelites at Gibeath Haaraloth.

As a leader, Joshua never second guessed the Lord and his commands. Who knows how many flint knives he would need to make to circumcise his whole nation of men, but he obeyed. Joshua's predecessor and mentor, Moses, had just been called by God to lead the people out of Egypt when God was ready to kill him for not having circumcised his son. (Exodus 20:24) Joshua, as Moses' successor, would have learned that lesson from Moses. Under Joshua's leadership, the people had promised to obey God and Joshua in all ways, which would have included circumcision.

Verse 4: Now this is why he did so: All those who came out of

Egypt—all the men of military age—died in the wilderness on the way after leaving Egypt.

Verse 6: The Israelites had moved about in the wilderness forty years until all the men who were of military age when they left Egypt had died, since they had not obeyed the Lord. For the Lord had sworn to them that they would not see the land he had solemnly promised their ancestors to give us, a land flowing with milk and honey.

Not only did the Lord promise good things for those who obeyed, God also swore (or vowed) not to bless those who disobeyed. His promises and vows concerning the land of Canaan (the Promised Land) extended over forty years. Today God's promises of salvation for those who believe in Jesus Christ, his son, extend to all people for eternity.

Verse 9: Then the Lord said to Joshua, "Today I have rolled away the reproach of Egypt from you." So the place has been called Gilgal to this day.

"Gilgal" in Hebrew is "to roll" or referring to "circle of stones". Gilgal is the place where the twelve stones were placed in a circle as a memorial. Here God has "rolled away" the past sufferings in Egypt and is ready to bless Israel with freedom in a land of richness. There is a city today still called Gilgal.

Verses 10-12: 10 On the evening of the fourteenth day of the month, while camped at Gilgal on the plains of Jericho, the Israelites celebrated the Passover. 11 The day after the Passover, that very day, they ate some of the produce of the land: unleavened bread and roasted grain. 12 The manna stopped the day after they ate this food from the land; there was no longer any manna for the Israelites, but that year they ate the produce of Canaan.

The Israelites continued their tradition of the Passover, as they had every year since they were in Egypt, but this Passover must have been historically celebratory. From the first Passover until this Passover, God had promised to spare them from death in Egypt and had promised Canaan to them. Not only were they celebrating in the site of the fulfilled promise of God after forty years, they could finally change their menu from heavenly manna and quail to the luscious handmade bread and roasted grain! What a feast for God and from God!

> Verse 13: Now when Joshua was near Jericho, he looked up and saw a man standing in front of him with a drawn sword in his hand. Joshua went up to him and asked, "Are you for us or for our enemies?"

Joshua showed courage, wisdom, and great leadership. Some may have drawn their swords in response to the gesture of the drawn sword in hand. Joshua wisely asked the important question first before acting: "Are you for us or against us?" How often do people attack others in defense before they know for certain whether they are friend or foe, or for certain whether they need to engage at all?

> Verse 14: "Neither," he replied, "but as commander of the army of the Lord I have now come." Then Joshua fell facedown to the ground in reverence, and asked him, "What message does my Lord have for his servant?"

Interesting that the commander of the Lord's army declares a neutral stance, being neither for Israel nor for Israel's enemies. The Lord is no one's enemy, neither is his army, which executes God's will. Joshua was in tune spiritually with God to know when he was in the presence of holiness as he fell to the ground in reverence to wait for God's word for him. As we long to hear from God, may we be ready spiritually to receive messages from God without hesitation.

> Verse 15: The commander of the Lord's army replied, "Take off your sandals, for the place where you are standing is holy." And Joshua did so.

This scene is reminiscent of Moses and the burning bush:

"Do not come any closer," God said. "Take off your sandals, for the place where you are standing is holy ground." 6 Then he said, "I am the God of your father,[a] the God of Abraham, the God of Isaac and the God of Jacob." At this, Moses hid his face, because he was afraid to look at God. — Exodus 3:5

Not only was Joshua following in Moses' footsteps, he was also invited to remove his sandals in a holy place and moment. However, instead of hearing God's voice in a burning bush, Joshua saw an actual warrior who is the commander of God's army. God was fighting Israel's battle with an actual army led by this figure of a man visible to Joshua. As the great leader that he was, Joshua fell to the ground in deference to a superior leader. As he stood up from this encounter, Joshua must have been encouraged to conquer Jericho in God's most unusual way.

Verses 10-11: 10 Now the priests who carried the ark remained standing in the middle of the Jordan until everything the Lord had commanded Joshua was done by the people, just as Moses had directed Joshua. The people hurried over, 11 and as soon as all of them had crossed, the ark of the Lord and the priests came to the other side while the people watched.

Reflection:

1. Do I need to commit or recommit myself or my children to the Lord? (perhaps in baptism rather than circumcision)

2. Moses and all the circumcised men were forbidden to enter the Promised Land because they disobeyed God. What blessing(s) have I missed because of a time when I lived in disobedience to God or when I only lived by my own rules? What consequences have I suffered because I did not listen to God's commandments and instructions?

3. The Lord told Joshua, "Today I have rolled away the shame of your slavery in Egypt." God rolled away the stone of shame on Calvary from Jesus' tomb. Jesus died and rose from the dead

to roll away the stones of our sins and shame. Have I accepted Jesus as my Savior and asked him to roll away my sins? If I have, do I harbor any residual shame from my past sins?

4. God's timing is perfect and fits our needs. How has God provided for my daily needs?

LEADERSHIP TIP #5: GREAT LEADERS COMMAND UNITY AND DEMAND LOYALTY.

Great leaders understand that all stakeholders need to have "skin in the game." Besides loyalty and trust, stakeholders have to buy into the mission and have something to gain for themselves or see value in their membership. In the case of Joshua's leadership, every Israelite had to be committed to their nation and tribe, and every Israelite had their sights set on the Promised Land, of which they would receive an inheritance. To be an Israelite required circumcision under God's law. Joshua had to build a new army of followers worthy of the mission to conquer and inherit the Promised Land, since the previous generation of circumcised men had perished in the wilderness. Under God's command, Joshua was to circumcise every adult male before continuing the conquest of the Promised Land. Even though the Jordan River miracle had intimidated the enemy, Joshua's followers had to be prepared for battle, and there was no more effective way to unify an army than for all of them to experience a "rite of passage" together. Ouch!

Response:

CHAPTER SIX

GREAT LEADERS ADAPT THEIR STRATEGY FOR THEIR PURPOSE

Summary:

Verse 2: Then the Lord said to Joshua, "See, I have delivered Jericho into your hands, along with its king and its fighting men.

Verse 3: March around the city once with all the armed men. Do this for six days.

Verse 4: Have seven priests carry trumpets of ram's horns in front of the ark. On the seventh day, march around the city seven times, with the priests blowing the trumpets.

The priests are crucial to the conquest of Jericho with trumpets made of rams' horns instead of weapons of war. At their signal, the whole army would shout and the wall of the city would collapse. These priests are from the family or tribe of Levi, who were loyal to God and Moses after the golden calf disaster in Exodus.

Verse 5: When you hear them sound a long blast on the trumpets, have the whole army give a loud shout; then the wall of the city will collapse and the army will go up, everyone straight in."

Verse 7: And he ordered the army, "Advance! March around the city, with an armed guard going ahead of the ark of the Lord."

This time, instead of the Ark of the Covenant leading the way, armed guards went ahead. This signaled that a battle would eventually ensue after they followed the unusual strategy of war commanded by God.

Verse 10: But Joshua had commanded the army, "Do not give a war cry, do not raise your voices, do not say a word until the day I tell you to shout. Then shout!"

The walls of Jericho were tightly secured with no one going in or out. The city was braced for the notorious Israelites. Instead of war whoops and battle cries, the people of Jericho watched the Israelites march around and around outside the city walls in complete silence. Imagine 40,000 soldiers, led by Joshua, marching in complete silence. Looking through the walls of

Jericho, the citizens of the city must have been confused by the repetitive rounds of marching warriors and the utter silence of this God-protected enemy.

> *Verse 16: The seventh time around, when the priests sounded the trumpet blast, Joshua commanded the army, "Shout! For the Lord has given you the city!*

Not cannon blasts, not the zing of fiery arrows, but the sound of people shouting caused the walls to fall. From an extended complete silence to the shouting of 40,000 warriors, those inside Jericho must have wondered if the deafening shouts and the shaking of the walls signaled an earthquake. They were already in meltdown from fear of Israel; this strategy must have rattled their nerves and shaken their courage to fight.

> *Verse 17: The city and all that is in it are to be devoted to the Lord. Only Rahab the prostitute and all who are with her in her house shall be spared, because she hid the spies we sent.*

As promised by the spies, Rahab and family were spared because of her mercy toward them.

> *Verses 18-19: 18 But keep away from the devoted things, so that you will not bring about your own destruction by taking any of them. Otherwise you will make the camp of Israel liable to destruction and bring trouble on it. 19 All the silver and gold and the articles of bronze and iron are sacred to the Lord and must go into his treasury."*

This conquest was the first in the Promised Land, and therefore, all the sacred items of metal belonged to the Lord as his first fruits. This is similar to tithing to the church; the first and best of the harvest (and plunder) always goes to the Lord. Those who disobeyed would be destroyed. This is similar to Ananias and Sapphira in Acts 5 when they held back their offering to God and lied about it. When their lie was exposed, they fell down and died at Peter's feet. In Joshua 7:1, only one man, Achan, would defy God's commands regarding Jericho, and he "paid for it" with his life and the life of his family.

> *Verse 21: They devoted the city to the Lord and destroyed with the sword every living thing in it—men and women, young and old, cattle, sheep and donkeys.*

> *Verse 23: So the young men who had done the spying went in and brought out Rahab, her father and mother, her brothers and sisters and all who belonged to her. They brought out her entire family and put them in a place outside the camp of Israel.*

Rahab and her family were saved from destruction and brought outside the walls of Jericho to live in peace near the camp of Israel.

> *Verse 24: Then they burned the whole city and everything in it, but they put the silver and gold and the articles of bronze and iron into the treasury of the Lord's house.*

In an act of complete obedience, the Israelites burned the whole place and its contents to the ground, except for the metals promised for the Lord's house. It must have been difficult to leave valuables to burn, but that was the command of God in exchange for their possession of the land.

> *Verse 26: At that time Joshua pronounced this solemn oath: "Cursed before the Lord is the one who undertakes to rebuild this city, Jericho.*

> *"At the cost of his firstborn son*
> *he will lay its foundations;*
> *at the cost of his youngest*
> *he will set up its gates."*

God had caused the walls of Jericho to tumble, and Joshua vowed that no one was to rebuild what God had destroyed. The penalty for disobedience for Pharaoh in Egypt was death to the firstborn. The penalty for disobedience in the Promised Land was death to the firstborn and to the youngest. Joshua double dares the people to go against God by vowing double deaths to the family of any man trying to rebuild Jericho.

This curse was fulfilled. See 1 Kings 16:34

In Ahab's time, Hiel of Bethel rebuilt Jericho. He laid its foundations at the cost of his firstborn son Abiram, and he set up its gates at the cost of his youngest son Segub, in accordance with the word of the Lord spoken by Joshua son of Nun.

Reflection:

1. In preparation for the victory over Jericho, there was a time designated for total silence and a time designated for the loudest shouting. When in my life have I had to remain silent and watch God work? What have I been asked to speak up in the name of the Lord for God's purposes to be fulfilled? Which was easier: keeping silent or speaking out?

2. Do I give the best of my first fruits to the Lord? Do I regularly tithe, giving up control of my offering for the work of God's kingdom?

3. How do my actions affect my children and grandchildren in both positive and negative ways? What do I need to change to stay in complete obedience to God and his Word?

LEADERSHIP TIP #6: GREAT LEADERS ADAPT THEIR STRATEGY FOR THEIR PURPOSE.

Great leaders leave themselves open to varying their strategies to accomplish their purpose. Not all leaders use the same strategies, nor does one leader use the same strategy for every purpose. To quote Clint Eastwood's Marine character in the movie Heartbreak Ridge, great leaders "improvise, adapt, and overcome".

Before the battle of Jericho, Joshua had used weapons for warfare. For Jericho, God commanded Joshua to use psychological warfare, using intimidation and fear prompted by the news that spread about the Israelites crossing the Jordan on dry ground. Additionally, Joshua and his army used a shock tactic of silent marching around the city, followed by the ram's horn blasts and shouting. Israelites were likely just as shocked as the people of Jericho to see the walls tumble down without a single person touching a rock, but the "Rock of Israel" worked another miracle for his people. In no war manual is there a strategy like the one used at Jericho, but spiritual leaders have replicated Joshua's Jericho strategy by marching around their churches or schools or homes seven times as they silently pray for spiritual breakthroughs, sometimes even blowing ram's horns and shouting praise on the seventh time around.

In my career as a public school administrator, whenever I was assigned to a different building, I would choose a Saturday when the building was closed and walk around the outside of the school seven times, silently praying for the staff, students, families, and visitors. I prayed for everyone's safety, spiritual growth, academic success, and my responsibility to be a worthy witness to God in all interactions and decisions. Sometimes on my Jericho walks, praying friends would join me and commit to praying for the school and for me all year long. There were challenging times when I thought back to those walks and trusted God to lead me. The Lord was faithful to be by my side every time.

Response:

_____

_____

_____

CHAPTER SEVEN

GREAT LEADERS MAKE TOUGH DECISIONS

Summary:

Verse 1: But the Israelites were unfaithful in regard to the devoted things; Achan son of Karmi, the son of Zimri, the son of Zerah, of the tribe of Judah, took some of them. So the Lord's anger burned against Israel.

The sin of one man affected the whole nation of Israel, and as a result, the whole nation was considered "unfaithful" by God.

Verse 2: Now Joshua sent men from Jericho to Ai, which is near Beth Aven to the east of Bethel, and told them, "Go up and spy out the region." So the men went up and spied out Ai. 3 When they returned to Joshua, they said, "Not all the army will have to go up against Ai. Send two or three thousand men to take it and do not weary the whole army, for only a few people live there." 4 So about three thousand went up; but they were routed by the men of Ai, 5 who killed about thirty-six of them. They chased the Israelites from the city gate as far as the stone quarries and struck them down on the slopes. At this the hearts of the people melted in fear and became like water.

From the spies' report, Joshua sent only two or three thousand men. Not knowing that there was sin among his people, and not knowing that the Lord was angry with them, Joshua lost the battle, lost 36 of his men, and his people lost their courage. What a turn of events for this Promised Land leader expecting victory over all the inhabitants! He had followed all of God's commands and was promised that the Lord would be at his side. He must have questioned himself and his leadership in his decisions that led to defeat in a battle over a town much smaller than Jericho.

Verses 6-7: Then Joshua tore his clothes and fell facedown to the ground before the ark of the Lord, remaining there till evening. The elders of Israel did the same, and sprinkled dust on their heads. 7 And Joshua said, "Alas, Sovereign Lord, why did you ever bring this people across the Jordan to deliver us into the hands of the Amorites to destroy us? If only we had been content to stay on the other side of the Jordan!

Joshua needed to regroup his people and himself. For the first time, as Joshua sought the Lord for answers, he started to sound like Moses and the people whining in the wilderness, asking God why and telling God that they would have been better off staying on the other side of the river. Joshua lost a physical battle, followed by losing a spiritual battle. However, in his humility and reverent posture, Joshua received truth, wisdom, and instructions from God that helped him to regroup, repurify, and rectify the situation.

> *Verses 10-12: The Lord said to Joshua, "Stand up! What are you doing down on your face? 11 Israel has sinned; they have violated my covenant, which I commanded them to keep. They have taken some of the devoted things; they have stolen, they have lied, they have put them with their own possessions. 12 That is why the Israelites cannot stand against their enemies; they turn their backs and run because they have been made liable to destruction. I will not be with you anymore unless you destroy whatever among you is devoted to destruction.*

Not only could the Israelites not stand against their enemies when sin was among them, but also God could not stand with Israel as long as sin existed. God needed them to be purified and prepared for future battles by purging the sin and the sinner.

> *Verse 13: "Go, consecrate the people. Tell them, 'Consecrate yourselves in preparation for tomorrow; for this is what the Lord, the God of Israel, says: There are devoted things among you, Israel. You cannot stand against your enemies until you remove them.*

The new marching orders from God for Joshua were to stand up, go, consecrate the people, and prepare for repairing the damage that had been done to the covenant between them and God. The "battle" had turned inward against the family member who had violated God's covenant. The conquest for the Promised Land could not move forward until the wrong was made right.

Verse 14: "'In the morning, present yourselves tribe by tribe. The tribe the Lord chooses shall come forward clan by clan; the clan the Lord chooses shall come forward family by family; and the family the Lord chooses shall come forward man by man. 15 Whoever is caught with the devoted things shall be destroyed by fire, along with all that belongs to him. He has violated the covenant of the Lord and has done an outrageous thing in Israel!'"

The Israelites would have remembered the golden calf disgrace in the wilderness that resulted in the guilty being killed by their kinsmen's swords. This punishment of death by fire was pronounced before the guilty party was identified. How terrifying for them all to know that death by fire was coming for family members! Is that not what we face today when we think of a future of heaven or hell for us and our family members? The difference is that today we have time to repent before the day of judgment comes for us, and each of us is responsible for our sins. Jesus died on the cross for our sins if we believe in him as our Lord. Jesus already paid the price; we need only to confess that we are sorry for our sins and proclaim Jesus as our Lord and Savior.

Verse 19: Then Joshua said to Achan, "My son, give glory to the Lord, the God of Israel, and honor him. Tell me what you have done; do not hide it from me."

In this plea for Achan to tell the truth, Joshua kept the focus on God and the importance of honoring the covenant. Then Joshua asked for Achan to tell him the truth, perhaps out of loyalty to him as leader, responsible to God for all the people's actions.

Verse 20: Achan replied, "It is true! I have sinned against the Lord, the God of Israel. This is what I have done: 21 When I saw in the plunder a beautiful robe from Babylonia, two hundred shekels of silver and a bar of gold weighing fifty shekels, I coveted them and took them. They are hidden in the ground inside my tent, with the silver underneath."

Dread for the sinner and his family; relief for the rest of the people that the truth was finally exposed.

Verses 22-23: 22 So Joshua sent messengers, and they ran to the tent, and there it was, hidden in his tent, with the silver underneath. 23 They took the things from the tent, brought them to Joshua and all the Israelites and spread them out before the Lord.

With the wisdom of a good leader, Joshua confirmed the verbal confession of Achan with the actual evidence and then showed them to the Lord.

Verse 24-25: 24 Then Joshua, together with all Israel, took Achan son of Zerah, the silver, the robe, the gold bar, his sons and daughters, his cattle, donkeys and sheep, his tent and all that he had, to the Valley of Achor. 25 Joshua said, "Why have you brought this trouble on us? The Lord will bring trouble on you today." Then all Israel stoned him, and after they had stoned the rest, they burned them.

This had to have been a difficult action for Joshua and the people, but not a difficult decision for Joshua as leader. Continuing in obedience to God, Joshua's decision had to match God's decision: death by stoning and fire.

Verse 26: Over Achan they heaped up a large pile of rocks, which remains to this day. Then the Lord turned from his fierce anger. Therefore that place has been called the Valley of Achor ever since.

Once the covenant had been repaired and restored, God and Joshua could move on to the next conquest together. The irony is in the contrast between the pile of stones from the Jordan River as a memorial of God's power to save and this pile of rocks as a memorial of God's power to destroy.

Reflection:

1. The Lord's anger burned against Israel because of Achan's sin, which resulted in the death of 36 men in the attempt to win the town of Ai. How does the sin of one person affect others in the world today? Does the Lord's anger burn against our nation

because of the sins of a few (or many)? What are we to do about it?

2. How have my sins affected those around me? How have I been affected by others' sins?

3. Joshua had stayed obedient to God, but one of his people had not. How did Joshua's responses to Achan's sin show Joshua's character and leadership?

4. Achan's stolen goods, his disobedience, and lies eventually were made known to everyone in the community. He could no longer hide from the truth and could no longer hide his stolen goods. What in my life needs to be made known or confessed to God? Am I hiding my sin(s) from others? from God? from myself?

5. Today we don't physically stone sinners to death, but are we guilty of "throwing stones" of judgment or criticism instead of letting God be the judge of all?

LEADERSHIP TIP #7: GREAT LEADERS MAKE TOUGH DECISIONS.

Leadership is easy when all is going well or as expected. However, when one person makes a mistake that impacts the entire group, great leaders make the tough decision to correct the individual to the level necessary to restore the group. In Achan's case, he made a fatal mistake, and once Joshua verified the truth of the matter, Achan had to go. One might say that Achan and his family were "stoned" and "fired" in the literal sense.

Even when a person makes a mistake that needs correction, redirection, and/or discipline, great leaders know how to speak the truth in love, not just to their followers in businesses and churches, but to their own family members. Followers accept the truth more readily from great leaders who are grounded in the truth of the Word of God, who walk in the faith, who lead by Godly example, who value relationships, and who communicate empathy and compassion. We see this in the exchange between Joshua and Achan; Joshua calls Achan "son" and asks for the truth, even when they both knew that the consequences would be severe.

When correcting a follower's mistake in today's world, a great leader does so with grace, understanding that all humans make mistakes. A great leader supports the person along the way, assisting where possible so that the mistake is not repeated. Making mistakes is how most of us learn; however, some people never learn, as in the case with Achan.

Response:

_____

_____

_____

_____

_____

_____

_____

_____

_____

CHAPTER EIGHT

GREAT LEADERS
ARE GREAT
COMMUNICATORS

Summary:

Verse 1: Then the Lord said to Joshua, "Do not be afraid; do not be discouraged. Take the whole army with you, and go up and attack Ai. For I have delivered into your hands the king of Ai, his people, his city and his land.

Joshua and the Israelites had regrouped from Achan's sins, and the covenant with God was restored. This time God commanded him to take the whole army to conquer Ai, not just two or three thousand, and the Lord promised victory over the king, his people, his city, and his land. When God gives us victory, he does it with completeness and wholeness.

Verse 2: You shall do to Ai and its king as you did to Jericho and its king, except that you may carry off their plunder and livestock for yourselves. Set an ambush behind the city."

For the second conquered city, the Israelites were permitted by God to keep all the plunder for themselves. Once we give our first fruits to God, he will surely bless us in return.

Verse 3-8: 3 So Joshua and the whole army moved out to attack Ai. He chose thirty thousand of his best fighting men and sent them out at night. 4 with these orders: "Listen carefully. You are to set an ambush behind the city. Don't go very far from it. All of you be on the alert. 5 I and all those with me will advance on the city, and when the men come out against us, as they did before, we will flee from them. 6 They will pursue us until we have lured them away from the city, for they will say, 'They are running away from us as they did before.' So when we flee from them, 7 you are to rise up from ambush and take the city. The Lord your God will give it into your hand. 8 When you have taken the city, set it on fire. Do what the Lord has commanded. See to it; you have my orders."

Joshua moved with his whole army on the second attempt at Ai, increasing the first flight from three thousand to thirty thousand fighting men and sending them out at night to prepare for an ambush. Great leader that he was, Joshua took the lead in advancing on the city and then created the illusion of retreat. As the enemy pursued them, the first flight of men ambushed the city and conquered it and set it on fire, as God had commanded.

Verse 13: So the soldiers took up their positions—with the main camp to the north of the city and the ambush to the west of it. That night Joshua went into the valley.

Verse 15: Joshua and all Israel let themselves be driven back before them, and they fled toward the wilderness.

Verse 17: Not a man remained in Ai or Bethel who did not go after Israel. They left the city open and went in pursuit of Israel.

Verse 18: Then the Lord said to Joshua, "Hold out toward Ai the javelin that is in your hand, for into your hand I will deliver the city." So Joshua held out toward the city the javelin that was in his hand.

Compare this scene to that of Moses in Exodus 17 when Joshua led the Israel army to victory over the Amalekites:

The Amalekites came and attacked the Israelites at Rephidim. 9 Moses said to Joshua, "Choose some of our men and go out to fight the Amalekites. Tomorrow I will stand on top of the hill with the staff of God in my hands." 10 So Joshua fought the Amalekites as Moses had ordered, and Moses, Aaron and Hur went to the top of the hill. 11 As long as Moses held up his hands, the Israelites were winning, but whenever he lowered his hands, the Amalekites were winning. 12 When Moses' hands grew tired, they took a stone and put it under him and he sat on it. Aaron and Hur held his hands up—one on one side, one on the other—so that his hands remained steady till sunset. 13 So Joshua overcame the Amalekite army with the sword. — Exodus 17:8-13

As the leader of Israel, Moses had his staff in hand while two men held up his hands as he watched Joshua defeat the

Amalekites. As the next leader of Israel, Joshua held his javelin in hand, standing on his own, leading his army to defeat Ai, and finally impaling the king on a pole with the help of the King of Heaven.

> *Verse 22: Those in the ambush also came out of the city against them, so that they were caught in the middle, with Israelites on both sides. Israel cut them down, leaving them neither survivors nor fugitives.*

> *Verse 26: For Joshua did not draw back the hand that held out his javelin until he had destroyed all who lived in Ai.*

> *Verse 29: He impaled the body of the king of Ai on a pole and left it there until evening. At sunset, Joshua ordered them to take the body from the pole and throw it down at the entrance of the city gate. And they raised a large pile of rocks over it, which remains to this day.*

Surely, after God had repeatedly told Joshua to "be strong and of good courage", Joshua must have felt an increase in his faith, strength, and courage when the Lord told him to hold out his javelin in his hand, into which God would deliver the city. Surely Joshua would have recalled his victory over the Amalekites and knew with certainty that the battle was the Lord's. Surely Joshua would have glanced up to the hills from the valley near Ai and imagined his predecessor on the hill with his hands raised.

Just as rocks were piled over the dead bodies of Achan and his family, rocks were piled over the dead body of the king of Ai, a memorial of God's power of destruction and of God's power of salvation.

> *Verses 30-31: 30 Then Joshua built on Mount Ebal an altar to the Lord, the God of Israel, 31 as Moses the servant of the Lord had commanded the Israelites. He built it according to what is written in the Book of the Law of Moses—an altar of uncut stones, on which no iron tool had been used. On it they offered to the Lord burnt offerings and sacrificed fellowship offerings.*

Unlike manmade materials, handcrafted metal, cut gemstones, or other artificial designs that glorified and memorialized humans as deities, God's altar was to be made of natural uncut God-created stones, according to the Book of the Law of Moses, given by God to man.

Verse 32: There, in the presence of the Israelites, Joshua wrote on stones a copy of the law of Moses.

This was a third stone "copy" of the commandments engraved in stone. God inscribed the first two sets, and then Joshua inscribed this set. As a transparent and obedient leader surpassing other leaders in strength and integrity, Joshua copied the law of Moses on the stones of the altar intentionally in the presence of all the people. Just as the Israelites had learned from Achan's sin that they all have responsibility to keep God's covenant, the people witnessed another copy of God's law etched in stone by their leader. Joshua ensured that no one would be exempt from "knowing" the words of the law and the conditions of the covenant.

Verse 33: All the Israelites, with their elders, officials and judges, were standing on both sides of the ark of the covenant of the Lord, facing the Levitical priests who carried it. Both the foreigners living among them and the native-born were there. Half of the people stood in front of Mount Gerizim and half of them in front of Mount Ebal, as Moses the servant of the Lord had formerly commanded when he gave instructions to bless the people of Israel.

Verse 34: Afterward, Joshua read all the words of the law—the blessings and the curses—just as it is written in the Book of the Law.

Under Joshua's leadership, the people read the law of Moses as Joshua carved the words on the stone altar. Then they listened to all the words of the law read to them by Joshua, both blessings and curses. Joshua delivered the law in written and spoken word, lest any one claim ignorance of the law.

Verse 35: There was not a word of all that Moses had commanded that Joshua did not read to the whole assembly of Israel, including the women and children, and the foreigners who lived among them.

Comprehensively, Joshua read the law of Moses to all the people, not just to the elders, not just to the men, but to all, including the marginalized of society—women, children, and foreigners among them.

We, like the Israelites, cannot claim that we don't know the truth.

Reflection:

1. Who have been my mentor leaders that have encouraged me or motivated me when I need it most? Under what circumstances do I rely on their examples?

2. Of deceased leaders who have impacted my life, which ones still come to mind? When? Why?

3. What images of strong spiritual leaders stick in my mind the most?

4. Did I realize that there was a third time in scripture when God's laws were engraved in stone? When is it important for me to see and hear the word of God for myself?

LEADERSHIP TIP #8: GREAT LEADERS ARE GREAT COMMUNICATORS.

Joshua gave specific communications to his army for the attack on Ai. He would create the impression that he and his men were retreating to get the men from Ai to leave their city and follow him. Then 30,000 other men ambushed the city. In order for this strategy to work, Joshua would have had to communicate very clearly to thousands of people. Clear communication brings clear results.

After the city of Ai fell into their hands, Joshua built an altar to

God at Mt. Ebal with uncut stone. Then Joshua himself cut the words of the law of Moses into the altar in the presence of the people. Afterward, Joshua himself read the entire law to all of the people: men, women, children, native-born, and foreigners. Joshua himself communicated the law in both written and spoken form, so that no one could give the excuse of not knowing what was expected of them by their leader.

Poor communication by leaders causes those that follow to be confused about what they should do. When followers make mistakes due to poor communication, poor leaders respond either by reprimanding them or removing them rather than holding themselves accountable. Great leaders give concise, clear, specific messages and afterwards, take responsibility for the effectiveness of their delivery by checking with their followers for their understanding of the leaders' messages.

Response:

_____

_____

_____

_____

_____

_____

_____

_____

CHAPTER NINE

GREAT LEADERS KEEP THEIR WORD AND KEEP THE PEACE

Summary:

Verses 1-2: 1 Now when all the kings west of the Jordan heard about these things—the kings in the hill country, in the western foothills, and along the entire coast of the Mediterranean Sea as far as Lebanon (the kings of the Hittites, Amorites, Canaanites, Perizzites, Hivites and Jebusites)— 2 they came together to wage war against Joshua and Israel.

The kings thought that their strategy of unity in war would help them to defeat Joshua and Israel. They didn't know the power of the Almighty God of Israel. The battles would be won based not upon how many, but who had the most power.

Verses 3-6: 3 However, when the people of Gibeon heard what Joshua had done to Jericho and Ai, 4 they resorted to a ruse: They went as a delegation whose donkeys were loaded with worn-out sacks and old wineskins, cracked and mended. 5 They put worn and patched sandals on their feet and wore old clothes. All the bread of their food supply was dry and moldy. 6 Then they went to Joshua in the camp at Gilgal and said to him and the Israelites, "We have come from a distant country; make a treaty with us."

Instead of a strategy of unity, the Gibeonites tried poor mouthing their way into a treaty, which worked because the Israelites forgot to check with God first.

Verse 14: The Israelites sampled their provisions but did not inquire of the Lord. 15 Then Joshua made a treaty of peace with them to let them live, and the leaders of the assembly ratified it by oath.

Just as all the Israelites were responsible to keep God's covenant, they were also all responsible for letting the Gibeonites deceive them into making a peace treaty with them without inquiring of the Lord beforehand. Even Joshua and his leaders were deceived by the contrived evidence of dry, moldy bread and cracked wineskins.

Verses 16-18: 16 Three days after they made the treaty with the

Gibeonites, the Israelites heard that they were neighbors, living near them. 17 So the Israelites set out and on the third day came to their cities: Gibeon, Kephirah, Beeroth and Kiriath Jearim. 18 But the Israelites did not attack them, because the leaders of the assembly had sworn an oath to them by the Lord, the God of Israel.

Though they erred in their human discernment about Gibeon, Joshua and the Israelites honored their oath sworn before God to live in peace with them. How admirable that they kept their word, even to liars. However, the lies came with consequences. The Gibeonites could live, but they would serve the whole assembly. Ironically, the Israelites come out of captivity and slavery to make another group of people their servants.

Verse 21: They continued, "Let them live, but let them be woodcutters and water carriers in the service of the whole assembly." So the leaders' promise to them was kept.

Their consequence doesn't sound as backbreaking as brick making, and the Israelites must have trusted them to carry their water without contaminating it. As we learn from God's covenant, a promise is a promise, and a great leader's promise is kept, presumably forever.

Verse 27: That day he made the Gibeonites woodcutters and water carriers for the assembly, to provide for the needs of the altar of the Lord at the place the Lord would choose. And that is what they are to this day.

While the Israelites were once enslaved to Pharaoh in Egypt, the Gibeonites were enslaved to serve the Lord by providing for the needs of the Lord's altar. The penalty of serving the Lord's altar "to this day" was merciful, compared to what was supposed to have happened to them by Joshua's army.

"Humans often forget where they came from. Instead of showing grace, we often want to reprimand others in ways that we had to endure ourselves." —Debbie Day

Reflection:

1. When have I gone ahead of the Lord in an important decision and regretted not praying to God about it first?

2. When have I asked mercy from God and received it?

3. When have I shown mercy to someone else, whether deserving or undeserving?

4. Is it difficult to trust someone who has lied to me before? How do I restore trust in them?

5. To what lengths would I go to save my life if I thought I was in extreme danger?

6. What promise or covenant have I kept that has been difficult but necessary for integrity's sake?

7. Is there any promise or "peace treaty" that I have made for which I now regret? How am I dealing with that?

LEADERSHIP TIP #9: GREAT LEADERS KEEP THEIR WORD AND KEEP THE PEACE.

Joshua made a bad deal with the Gibeonites. He thought that he had checked out their story by inspecting their cracked wineskins, moldy bread, worn out shoes, and patched clothing. He had not consulted God about this decision; it seemed to be a no-brainer. He was outsmarted. Even though he made a vow to these deceitful people, Joshua kept his vow and did not destroy them.

However, he made a way to honor his word and negotiate an additional term of the treaty: they had to be the water carriers and wood cutters who would serve the Lord's altar. Joshua turned a bad deal into a good way to honor God.

Response:

_____

_____

_____

_____

_____

_____

_____

_____

_____

_____

_____

_____

_____

_____

_____

CHAPTER TEN

GREAT LEADERS ARE GREAT ENCOURAGERS

Summary:

Verses 5-6: Then the five kings of the Amorites—the kings of Jerusalem, Hebron, Jarmuth, Lachish and Eglon—joined forces. They moved up with all their troops and took up positions against Gibeon and attacked it. 6 The Gibeonites then sent word to Joshua in the camp at Gilgal: "Do not abandon your servants. Come up to us quickly and save us! Help us, because all the Amorite kings from the hill country have joined forces against us."

Had the Israelites not formed a peace pact with the Gibeonites and made servants of them, the Israelites would have conquered and plundered Gibeon. Instead, because they mistakenly vowed to be at peace with Gibeon, the Israelites were put into the position of defending them from five Amorite kings, who joined forces against Gibeon. True to their word, Joshua and his warriors came to their aid with God's promise of victory over them all.

Verse 8: The Lord said to Joshua, "Do not be afraid of them; I have given them into your hand. Not one of them will be able to withstand you."

Once again God encouraged Joshua not to be afraid and told him that he would stand strong against the enemy.

Verse 9: After an all-night march from Gilgal, Joshua took them by surprise.

Joshua had the military strategy of moving and fighting at night with surprise attacks. In our spiritual warfare, prayers and praise in the middle of the night can be just as effective as talking to God and worshiping during the daylight. For God, victory in battle takes place night and day.

Verse 10: The Lord threw them into confusion before Israel, so Joshua and the Israelites defeated them completely at Gibeon. Israel pursued them along the road going up to Beth Horon and cut them down all the way to Azekah and Makkedah.

Again the word "completely" is used to describe God's victory for Joshua and Israel, lest there be any doubt about the outcome. God demonstrated his power to calm Joshua and the people; he also demonstrated how he can incite fear and confusion when needed to conquer the enemy. Imagine the power God gives us to be strong, courageous, calm, and strategic in our spiritual battles. Imagine, also, the power that God can use against our spiritual enemies of our souls.

> Verse 11: As they fled before Israel on the road down from Beth Horon to Azekah, the Lord hurled large hailstones down on them, and more of them died from the hail than were killed by the swords of the Israelites.

Who fought and won the battle at Gibeon? Joshua and his army fought with swords, but it was the Lord who killed most of the enemy by large hailstones, should anyone be tempted to boast about their prowess in war. God will always get the honor and glory for the things he has done.

> Verse 12: On the day the Lord gave the Amorites over to Israel, Joshua said to the Lord in the presence of Israel:"Sun, stand still over Gibeon, and you, moon, over the Valley of Aijalon."

> Verse 13: So the sun stood still, and the moon stopped,
> till the nation avenged itself on its enemies, as it is written in the Book of Jashar.

The sun stopped in the middle of the sky and delayed going down for about a full day.

Impressive as the hail storm was in killing most of the Amorite soldiers, God worked yet another miracle for Joshua by stopping time. Joshua asked for and received another full day of daylight. He still had to finish off the rest of the enemy and their five kings. As was his leadership style, Joshua prayed for this miracle, not in private, but "in the presence of Israel" so that all his people would know whether or not God would answer his prayer.

Imagine hearing our spiritual leader pray for the sun to stand still, and it happens! That would be a powerful prayer, a powerful spiritual leader, and a powerful God. Would we believe it, or would we call it some sort of "scientific" anomaly of nature?

"This battle reminds me of the Six Day War that Israel fought in 1967. Before the Arab nations could strike, Israel launched preemptive airstrikes against Egyptian airfields. As the Israeli Air Force took to the sky, the first miracle of the war occurred. Jordanian radar detected the planes and tried to warn Egypt, but the Egyptians had changed their coding frequencies the previous day and had not yet updated the Jordanians with the new codes. The message never went through, giving Israel the element of surprise. That's just one of several miracles that took place, including a sandstorm that grounded enemy aircraft." — Debbie Day

Verse 16: Now the five kings had fled and hidden in the cave at Makkedah.

Verses 18-20: 18 he (Joshua) said, "Roll large rocks up to the mouth of the cave, and post some men there to guard it. 19 But don't stop; pursue your enemies! Attack them from the rear and don't let them reach their cities, for the Lord your God has given them into your hand." 20 So Joshua and the Israelites defeated them completely, but a few survivors managed to reach their fortified cities.

Strategically, Joshua was not distracted by the kings' attempted escape; he was not going to let the enemies escape; and even when some survivors managed to reach their cities, they would eventually be destroyed. (See verse 28.)

Verses 22-25: 22 Joshua said, "Open the mouth of the cave and bring those five kings out to me." 23 So they brought the five kings out of the cave—the kings of Jerusalem, Hebron, Jarmuth, Lachish and Eglon. 24 When they had brought these kings to Joshua, he summoned all the men of Israel and said to the army commanders who had come with him, "Come here and put your feet on the necks of these kings." So they came forward and placed their feet on their necks. 25 Joshua said to them, "Do not be afraid; do not be discouraged. Be strong and courageous. This is what the Lord will do to all the enemies you are going to fight."

What a powerful sight to imagine Joshua's army commanders with their feet on the kings' necks! What would be their consequence for coming against the servants of Israel? It was at this moment that Joshua needed to share a word of encouragement to his commanders about what was about to happen. Joshua used the same words that the Lord had repeatedly said to him: "Do not be afraid, do not be discouraged, be strong and courageous." These empowering words should be repeated daily to ourselves and to each other as we go into the world and fight our spiritual battles on a daily basis. The battle always belongs to the Lord.

Verses 26-28: 26 Then Joshua put the kings to death and exposed their bodies on five poles, and they were left hanging on the poles until evening. 27 At sunset Joshua gave the order and they took them down from the poles and threw them into the cave where they had been hiding. At the mouth of the cave they placed large rocks, which are there to this day. 28 That day Joshua took Makkedah. He put the city and its king to the sword and totally destroyed everyone in it. He left no survivors. And he did to the king of Makkedah as he had done to the king of Jericho.

Another pile of rocks for a grave, this time at the mouth of the cave for people to remember "to this day." Once again, Joshua left no survivors, and the word was out about the fate of any king who wanted to go against Israel.

Verse 29: Then Joshua and all Israel with him moved on from Makkedah to Libnah and attacked it.

Verse 32: The Lord gave Lachish into Israel's hands, and Joshua took it on the second day. The city and everyone in it he put to the sword, just as he had done to Libnah.

Verse 33: Meanwhile, Horam king of Gezer had come up to help Lachish, but Joshua defeated him and his army—until no survivors were left.

Verse 34: Then Joshua and all Israel with him moved on from Lachish to Eglon; they took up positions against it and attacked it.

Verse 36: Then Joshua and all Israel with him went up from Eglon to Hebron and attacked it.

Verse 38: Then Joshua and all Israel with him turned around and attacked Debir.

In a single military campaign to secure the Promised Land, Joshua and the Israelite army systematically conquered the following cities and "totally destroyed all who breathed":

- Makkedah
- Libnah
- Lachish
- King Horam of Gezer
- Eglon
- Hebron
- Debir

Verses 40-43: 40 So Joshua subdued the whole region, including the hill country, the Negev, the western foothills and the mountain slopes, together with all their kings. He left no survivors. He totally destroyed all who breathed, just as the Lord, the God of Israel, had commanded. 41 Joshua subdued them from Kadesh Barnea to Gaza and from the whole region of Goshen to Gibeon. 42 All these kings and their lands Joshua conquered in one campaign, because the Lord, the God of Israel, fought for Israel. 43 Then Joshua returned with all Israel to the camp at Gilgal.

Imagine back to God's promise to give the Israelites the Promised Land "flowing with milk and honey." I had imagined a return to a "Garden of Eden" full of fruits and green landscapes, when in reality, it was a full scale conquest of occupied territories with bloodshed and dead bodies everywhere.

Compare the conquest of Joshua in the Promised Land to the victory of Moses over Pharaoh and the Egyptian armies. There were also dead bodies of soldiers and horses everywhere.

Exodus 14:30 That day the Lord saved Israel from the hands of the Egyptians, and Israel saw the Egyptians lying dead on the shore.

The journey from Egypt to the occupation of the Promised Land was difficult, deadly, bloody, and sacrificial, but God was with them all the way. My imagined return to a new "Garden of Eden" will still happen; we will just have to wait awhile for Jesus to return.

Then the angel showed me the river of the water of life, as clear as crystal, flowing from the throne of God and of the Lamb 2 down the middle of the great street of the city. On each side of the river stood the tree of life, bearing twelve crops of fruit, yielding its fruit every month. And the leaves of the tree are for the healing of the nations. 3 No longer will there be any curse. The throne of God and of the Lamb will be in the city, and his servants will serve him. 4 They will see his face, and his name will be on their foreheads. 5 There will be no more night. They will not need the light of a lamp or the light of the sun, for the Lord God will give them light. And they will reign for ever and ever. —Revelation 22: 1-5

Reflection:

1. How can I begin every day feeling strong, courageous, calm, and encouraged, as God encouraged Joshua and Joshua encouraged his army commanders?

2. When facing challenges of the day, do I keep in mind that the battle belongs to the Lord?

3. What characteristics of Joshua's leadership style would I like to embrace in my leadership role(s)?

LEADERSHIP TIP #10: GREAT LEADERS ARE GREAT ENCOURAGERS.

Joshua was encouraged by the Lord many times to be strong and courageous. Even great leaders need to hear words of encouragement. In turn, Joshua gave these words of encouragement to all of his men and his army commanders when they had their feet on the four kings' necks. Following this victory, the Israelites would be in many more battles. Joshua used this opportunity within the context of this great victory, to encourage his men to continue fighting fearlessly with strength and courage because God would give them victory over all their other enemies.

Response:

_____

_____

_____

Response:

_____

_____

_____

_____

_____

_____

_____

_____

_____

_____

_____

_____

_____

_____

CHAPTER ELEVEN

GREAT LEADERS HAVE GREAT TIMING AND THINK QUICKLY

Summary:

Verses 1-3: 1 When Jabin king of Hazor heard of this, he sent word to Jobab king of Madon, to the kings of Shimron and Akshaph, 2 and to the northern kings who were in the mountains, in the Arabah south of Kinnereth, in the western foothills and in Naphoth Dor on the west; 3 to the Canaanites in the east and west; to the Amorites, Hittites, Perizzites and Jebusites in the hill country; and to the Hivites below Hermon in the region of Mizpah. 4 They came out with all their troops and a large number of horses and chariots—a huge army, as numerous as the sand on the seashore.

Israel's new group of adversaries joined northern forces described as coming from the north in the mountains to the south, from east to west, from hill country and below to form a huge army "as numerous as the sand on the seashore." Typically there is strength in numbers, but these forces did not have Israel's One True God on their side. The ominous description of the size of the armies would strike fear into the hearts of any warriors, but the Lord, once again, assured Joshua not to be afraid and to expect victory within a 24-hour period.

Verse 6: The Lord said to Joshua, "Do not be afraid of them, because by this time tomorrow I will hand all of them, slain, over to Israel. You are to hamstring their horses and burn their chariots."

Verse 7: So Joshua and his whole army came against them suddenly at the Waters of Merom and attacked them, 8 and the Lord gave them into the hand of Israel. They defeated them and pursued them all the way to Greater Sidon, to Misrephoth Maim, and to the Valley of Mizpah on the east, until no survivors were left.

God's military strategy used here by Joshua is the quick timing, as his entire army struck "suddenly", defeated and pursued their enemies until none was left.

Verse 11: Everyone in it they put to the sword. They totally destroyed them, not sparing anyone that breathed, and he burned Hazor itself.

This wave of Joshua's military victories came quickly and completely, again leaving no survivors

Verse 13: Yet Israel did not burn any of the cities built on their mounds—except Hazor, which Joshua burned.

It is significant to note that Joshua only burned the city whose king had started the war and united surrounding cities to join him–the city of Hazor. The rest of the cities were spared, perhaps because they were positioned securely on mounds rather than by walls, or perhaps because they were of value to Israel's occupation and habitation. Regardless of the reason for sparing or burning, the following verses clarify that Joshua was following the commands of Moses, who had followed the commands of the Lord.

Verse 15: As the Lord commanded his servant Moses, so Moses commanded Joshua, and Joshua did it; he left nothing undone of all that the Lord commanded Moses.

Verse 20: For it was the Lord himself who hardened their hearts to wage war against Israel, so that he might destroy them totally, exterminating them without mercy, as the Lord had commanded Moses.

As often as one may think of God as a God of mercy, in the case of the enemies of Israel, God showed no mercy at all to the point of their extinction.

Verses 21-23: 21 At that time Joshua went and destroyed the Anakites from the hill country: from Hebron, Debir and Anab, from all the hill country of Judah, and from all the hill country of Israel. Joshua totally destroyed them and their towns. 22 No Anakites were left in Israelite territory; only in Gaza, Gath and Ashdod did any survive. 23 So Joshua took the entire land, just as the Lord had directed Moses, and he gave it as an inheritance to Israel according to their tribal divisions. Then the land had rest from war.

Whether the burning of cities and utter destruction of the

enemy was considered a sacrifice to God or God's purification of the land for his people to inhabit anew, the Promised Land was flowing with blood and bodies before Israel could enjoy its flow of milk and honey. Finally the land and the people could rest from war.

Reflection:

1. Have I ever had an experience of needing to take sudden action, which resulted in immediate success because of God's favor and assurance?

2. Have I ever needed to wait, sometimes for a long time, to take action, which resulted in success because of God's favor and assurance?

3. Adversaries can come against me in terms of size, strength,or numbers, but do I ever need to worry about my enemies, if God is on my side? How can I be sure that God is on my side in life's "battles"?

4. In leadership, when have I taken godly advice from my predecessor in a situation, which brought me success?

5. What land, territories, powers, scope of influence, or special possessions has God given to me as his inheritance, according to his promises? How am I to use them today for the preservation of God's promises for my descendants?

6. Has God ever asked me (in a metaphorical or physical way) to "burn" or "completely destroy" something of mine? Have I ever purged anything from my life in order to be more fully devoted to God?

7. What can I do personally to bring about rest to my land, to my family, to my world? What would God have me to do for peace in the land?

LEADERSHIP TIP #11: GREAT LEADERS HAVE GREAT TIMING AND THINK QUICKLY.

His enemies formed a united front and became as "numerous as sand on the seashore". Joshua had to jump into action and mobilize his whole army as one unit to attack swiftly. They had to appear bigger, stronger, and faster. Perhaps he chose to fight near the Waters of Merom because it was the first time he spotted the enemy. Or perhaps he chose to fight near a large body of water because his enemies would have heard of God's power over water to save his people: at the river Jordan and at the Red Sea. More psychological warfare? Perhaps.

"This is what is called 'in game' managing. It's what makes good coaches. I happen to believe it's something that can't be easily taught. I think a person has to have the talent or the anointing for it. Jesus told the disciples not to worry about how to answer their adversaries, that the Holy Spirit would tell them what to do in the moment. Good leaders need to follow the Holy Spirit's leading by responding quickly and confidently. which in turn instills confidence in their leadership abilities by those who follow them." – Debbie Day

Response:

_____

_____

_____

_____

_____

CHAPTER TWELVE

GREAT LEADERS ARE ACCOUNTABLE AND KEEP GREAT RECORDS

Summary:

Verse 1: These are the kings of the land whom the Israelites had defeated and whose territory they took over east of the Jordan, from the Arnon Gorge to Mount Hermon, including all the eastern side of the Arabah:

Verses 6: Moses, the servant of the Lord, and the Israelites conquered them. And Moses the servant of the Lord gave their land to the Reubenites, the Gadites and the half-tribe of Manasseh to be their possession.

Verse 7: Here is a list of the kings of the land that Joshua and the Israelites conquered on the west side of the Jordan, from Baal Gad in the Valley of Lebanon to Mount Halak, which rises toward Seir. Joshua gave their lands as an inheritance to the tribes of Israel according to their tribal divisions.

Verse 24: Thirty-one kings in all were defeated by Moses and Joshua, as commanded by God and fought by the twelve tribes of Israel!

Reflection:

1. What has been my greatest victory in my life?

2. With whom have I fought and won spiritual battles with the help of God?

3. What words of encouragement from God (and others) keep me fighting my battles every day?

LEADERSHIP TIP #12: GREAT LEADERS ARE ACCOUNTABLE AND KEEP GREAT RECORDS.

Joshua kept record of all the victories east of the Jordan, west of the Jordan, and those of Moses. Recorded are the defeated kings and the division of lands as the inheritance to the tribes of Israel. Keeping good records helps with past history, future planning, and decision making. Keeping records of victories builds faith in past and present leaders. Keeping records of what God has done for his people builds our faith to help us through times when our faith is tested.

Response:

_____

_____

_____

_____

_____

_____

_____

_____

_____

_____

_____

_____

CHAPTER THIRTEEN

GREAT LEADERS STAY ON COURSE AND COMPLETE THE JOB

Summary:

Verse 1: When Joshua had grown old, the Lord said to him, "You are now very old, and there are still very large areas of land to be taken over.

Joshua was not finished yet, even though he had grown old. There was still work to do in order for God to fulfill his promise to his people.

Verse 6: "As for all the inhabitants of the mountain regions from Lebanon to Misrephoth Maim, that is, all the Sidonians, I myself will drive them out before the Israelites. Be sure to allocate this land to Israel for an inheritance, as I have instructed you, 7 and divide it as an inheritance among the nine tribes and half of the tribe of Manasseh."

Verse 14: But to the tribe of Levi he gave no inheritance, since the food offerings presented to the Lord, the God of Israel, are their inheritance, as he promised them.

Verse 15: This verse describes the land that Moses had given to the tribe of Reuben, according to its clans:

Verse 24: This verse describes the land that Moses had given to the tribe of Gad, according to its clans:

Verse 29: This verse describes the land that Moses had given to the half-tribe of Manasseh, that is, to half the family of the descendants of Manasseh, according to its clans:

Moses had already allocated the land east of the Jordan River to the tribes of Reuben, Gad, and the half-tribe of Manasseh. For the land west of the Jordan, Joshua was to finish taking over the rest of the Promised Land and allocating it to the nine and a half tribes there.

Verse 33: But to the tribe of Levi, Moses had given no inheritance; the Lord, the God of Israel, is their inheritance, as he promised them.

In exchange for being given no land as their allotment, the Levites were given God as their inheritance. They would be given towns to live in, pasturelands for their flocks and livestock (see 14:4), and fed by the food offerings presented to God by the rest of the Israelites through future generations.

Reflection:

1. Have I ever felt old and realized that God wasn't finished with me yet–that there was still work to do for him?

2. Do I know older people in my life who are still going strong in the kingdom of God?

3. In Scripture, does God have a retirement plan on earth for any of his people? What is God's ultimate retirement plan for all of his people?

4. If I had a choice, would I prefer to be a Levite with no land ownership, but access to a place to live, pastureland, and all the food offerings to God for generations to come? Or would I prefer to own an allotment of land for my tribe and future generations?

5. What will be the spiritual inheritance that I leave for my future generations?

6. What has God promised to me?

LEADERSHIP TIP #13: GREAT LEADERS STAY ON COURSE AND COMPLETE THE JOB.

God had to have a chat with Joshua to remind him that he wasn't getting any younger and that there was still work to be done. God reminded him to be sure to allocate the land as instructed.

In our culture, leaders don't need to be reminded of their age or that they are growing old, but at times great leaders take an account of what has been accomplished and what still needs to be completed in order to reach their goals.

"Our culture does not honor older people like other cultures do. There seems to be almost a war of the generations such as the Millennials vs. the Boomers. Older people are considered irrelevant, which personally makes it hard to stay motivated to continue to make a difference in our current world. The fact that God reminded Joshua he was old, but at the same time told him to get on with his goals, inspires me to keep on. I pray for opportunities and open doors to serve God with what I am equipped to offer."
— Debbie Day

Response:

CHAPTER FOURTEEN

GREAT LEADERS REMEMBER THEIR ROOTS

Summary:

Verse 2: Their inheritances were assigned by lot to the nine and a half tribes, as the Lord had commanded through Moses.

Verse 4: for Joseph's descendants had become two tribes— Manasseh and Ephraim. The Levites received no share of the land but only towns to live in, with pasturelands for their flocks and herds.

Verse 6: Now the people of Judah approached Joshua at Gilgal, and Caleb son of Jephunneh the Kenizzite said to him, "You know what the Lord said to Moses the man of God at Kadesh Barnea about you and me. 7 I was forty years old when Moses the servant of the Lord sent me from Kadesh Barnea to explore the land. And I brought him back a report according to my convictions, 9 So on that day Moses swore to me, 'The land on which your feet have walked will be your inheritance and that of your children forever, because you have followed the Lord my God wholeheartedly.' 10 "Now then, just as the Lord promised, he has kept me alive for forty-five years since the time he said this to Moses, while Israel moved about in the wilderness. So here I am today, eighty-five years old! 11 I am still as strong today as the day Moses sent me out; I'm just as vigorous to go out to battle now as I was then. 12 Now give me this hill country that the Lord promised me that day. You yourself heard then that the Anakites were there and their cities were large and fortified, but, the Lord helping me, I will drive them out just as he said."

Caleb is not quoted often in Scripture, the first was when Joshua and Caleb were the only two of the ten spies who advised Moses to go and take possession of the Promised Land. The rest of the spies were afraid of the size and scope of their enemies. Forty-year-old Caleb spoke of his convictions to Moses, who listened to him and followed his and Joshua's advice.

"The people who live there are powerful, and the cities are fortified and very large. We even saw descendants of Anak

there. 33 We seemed like grasshoppers in our own eyes, and we looked the same to them." — Numbers 13:28, 33: 28

Caleb had already explored the land of Anak when he was a spy for Moses before Israel crossed the Jordan River. He was familiar with the challenges that were ahead and was ready to proceed with faith and courage because he knew that the Lord had promised him the land.

Then Caleb silenced the people before Moses and said, "We should go up and take possession of the land, for we can certainly do it." — Numbers 13:30

From spy to warrior, Caleb fought in Joshua's army, conquering Jericho, Ai, and many more. Eighty-five-year-old Caleb spoke up as he and his tribe of Judah approached the leader of Israel, this time Joshua, to ask for the hill country that was promised to him by the Lord and Moses. Caleb reminded Joshua of their partnership as former spies for Moses, and recounted the promise of land by Moses. Caleb acknowledged that he was just as vigorous at 85 as he was at 40 and asked for Joshua's blessing on conquering the large and fortified cities inhabited by the Anakites. After listening to Caleb's respectful, factual, convincing plea, Joshua granted Caleb his request, blessed him, and gave him his inheritance. Whether the timing was right for Joshua, or Caleb had waited for the right time to ask for what was rightfully his, the two agreed to Caleb's proposal.

Verse 13: Then Joshua blessed Caleb son of Jephunneh and gave him Hebron as his inheritance.

Reflection:

1. What do I need to do to follow God "wholeheartedly" like Caleb?

2. What people do I know who seldomly speak up to a leader, but when they do, their words are respectful, factual, timely, convincing, and effective?

3. What difference was there in 40-year-old Caleb vs. 85-year-old Caleb? What had he experienced in those 45 years? Why is it important to keep up our strength and skills as we grow older?

4. When have I had to be courageous in speaking against popular opinion about an important decision to be made? specifically in my life? at my work? at church?

5. Have I ever had a friend or peer get promoted and become my boss or supervisor? How did I handle that transition? How did my friend or peer respond?

6. How long would I be willing to wait to claim something that was promised to me by a leader? By God? What is the benefit of waiting or not waiting?

LEADERSHIP TIP #14: GREAT LEADERS REMEMBER THEIR ROOTS.

Great leaders never forget who helped them get to where they are. After 45 years, Caleb went before Joshua and asked for his inheritance, a place that still needed to be conquered, a place of the giant, formidable Anakites that they had seen when they explored the Promised Land for Moses. Caleb reminded Joshua of what the Lord and Moses had said to the both of them. They were promised land, and Caleb wanted Joshua to make good on the promise from God through Moses. Joshua listened to Caleb's request, honored him with his own city of Hebron, and blessed him. Surely there was some talk of their "good old days" when they were spies and went against all the other spies in their report to Moses. Good times. Note that Joshua had not yet received his own inheritance, but granted Caleb his upon his request.

"Just as roots in a tree function to anchor it to keep it strong through storms and other assaults, relying on one's roots can keep a leader strong." — Debbie Day

"The devil will try to tell us that we are not able to carry out God's work when we allow him to by not striving to stay strong. Our gifts atrophy when we cease to use them." — Debbie Day

Response:

_____

_____

_____

_____

_____

_____

_____

_____

_____

_____

_____

_____

CHAPTER FIFTEEN

GREAT LEADERS RECOGNIZE LIMITATIONS OF THEIR PEOPLE

Summary:

Verses 1-12: Boundaries set and allotted for Judah

Verses 13-19: Boundaries set and allotted for Caleb

Verses 21-62: Boundaries for southern towns of Judah

Verse 63: Judah could not dislodge the Jebusites, who were living in Jerusalem; to this day the Jebusites live there with the people of Judah

For most other territories, God commanded complete destruction of the inhabitants. Jerusalem could not be totally conquered, so the people of Judah live alongside the Jebusites.

Reflection:

1. What could be possible repercussions for not completely dislodging the Jebusites?

2. There is no report of a peace treaty, as with the Gibeonites, who served as woodcutters and water carriers for the Israelites. Because Israel could not dislodge the Jebusites, what accommodations or concessions would have to have been made?

3. What is the significance of Jerusalem being the city that was not totally conquered by Israel? Is there any prophecy or foreshadowing suggested here?

LEADERSHIP TIP #15: GREAT LEADERS RECOGNIZE LIMITATIONS OF THEIR PEOPLE.

God's orders were for the inhabitants to be completely removed or destroyed by Joshua and his army. This did not always happen, and Joshua's report stated that Judah could not dislodge the Jebusites, so they cohabitated. Apparently, Joshua took no further action nor gave further orders for Judah. Note that Judah was the tribe of Joshua's old spying buddy, Caleb. Great leaders recognize that people have limitations.

"The failure to dislodge the Jebusites was one that caused a lot of future pain. God's people were repeatedly influenced by that pagan culture and turned to Baal worship later on. David conquered it later, but even to this day, there is perhaps no greater contested city than Jerusalem.

"Joshua delegated a task to the people of Judah, but they were limited in their abilities and failed. He recognized their limitations and accepted their solution to live with a subdued people.

"God wants the best for us, but sometimes our failures limit his blessings on us." – Chad P. Shepherd

Response:

_____

_____

_____

_____

_____

_____

_____

_____

CHAPTER SIXTEEN

GREAT LEADERS UNDERSTAND THAT LIFE IS NOT FAIR

Summary:

Verses 1-4: The allotment for Joseph began at the Jordan, east of the springs of Jericho, and went up from there through the desert into the hill country of Bethel. 2 It went on from Bethel (that is, Luz), crossed over to the territory of the Arkites in Ataroth, 3 descended westward to the territory of the Japhletites as far as the region of Lower Beth Horon and on to Gezer, ending at the Mediterranean Sea. 4 So Manasseh and Ephraim, the descendants of Joseph, received their inheritance.

Verses 5-10: This was the territory of Ephraim, according to its clans:

The boundary of their inheritance went from Ataroth Addar in the east to Upper Beth Horon 6 and continued to the Mediterranean Sea. From Mikmethath on the north it curved eastward to Taanath Shiloh, passing by it to Janoah on the east. 7 Then it went down from Janoah to Ataroth and Naarah, touched Jericho and came out at the Jordan. 8 From Tappuah the border went west to the Kanah Ravine and ended at the Mediterranean Sea. This was the inheritance of the tribe of the Ephraimites, according to its clans. 9 It also included all the towns and their villages that were set aside for the Ephraimites within the inheritance of the Manassites.10 They did not dislodge the Canaanites living in Gezer; to this day the Canaanites live among the people of Ephraim but are required to do forced labor.

If the inhabitants of Gibeon and Ephraim were not destroyed, they were forced to work for Israel. These details were significant enough to go on record in the book of Joshua. However, there is no report in the book of Joshua of the Jebusites being forced to work for Israel when they were conquered by the tribe of Judah. Note that the capital of the Jebusites was the city of Jerusalem. What could that mean for the future of Jerusalem and the Israelites living there?

Reflection:

1. How difficult is it to live with two families under one roof, related or non-related? How difficult must it have been for one nation to cohabitate with another nation?

2. Following the continual war over the Holy Land and the Gaza strip, how can we trace the roots of this conflict back to biblical times?

3. When have I struggled with setting boundaries, either physically or emotionally with other people? What strategies do I use to hold to these boundaries?

LEADERSHIP TIP #16: GREAT LEADERS UNDERSTAND THAT LIFE IS NOT FAIR.

The record shows that the Gibeonite and Ephraimite survivors were required to do forced labor, but there is no record of the same outcome for Jebusite survivors living in Jerusalem. The people of Judah "lived alongside" the Jebusites. Does this have anything to do with Caleb belonging to Judah's tribe, and Joshua did not insist? What we learn from great leaders, and every mom who ever lived, is that "life is not fair."

Response:

_____

_____

_____

_____

_____

_____

_____

_____

_____

_____

_____

_____

_____

_____

_____

_____

_____

_____

_____

CHAPTER SEVENTEEN

GREAT LEADERS CAN BE MEN OR WOMEN

Summary:

Verses 1-2: allotment for the tribe of Manasseh as Joseph's firstborn

Verses 3-6: Now Zelophehad son of Hepher, the son of Gilead, the son of Makir, the son of Manasseh, had no sons but only daughters, whose names were Mahlah, Noah, Hoglah, Milkah and Tirzah. 4 They went to Eleazar the priest, Joshua son of Nun, and the leaders and said, "The Lord commanded Moses to give us an inheritance among our relatives." So Joshua gave them an inheritance along with the brothers of their father, according to the Lord's command. 5 Manasseh's share consisted of ten tracts of land besides Gilead and Bashan east of the Jordan, 6 because the daughters of the tribe of Manasseh received an inheritance among the sons. The land of Gilead belonged to the rest of the descendants of Manasseh.

Since a son of Manasseh had no sons, the daughters spoke up for their inheritance, which Joshua granted. For women who were typically treated as property, Joshua's decision legitimized the ownership of land by women. However, the Lord commanded Moses to require the female landowners of Manasseh to marry within their own tribe to maintain the original divisions of land.

Then at the Lord's command Moses gave this order to the Israelites: "What the tribe of the descendants of Joseph is saying is right. 6 This is what the Lord commands for Zelophehad's daughters: They may marry anyone they please as long as they marry within their father's tribal clan. 7 No inheritance in Israel is to pass from one tribe to another, for every Israelite shall keep the tribal inheritance of their ancestors. 8 Every daughter who inherits land in any Israelite tribe must marry someone in her father's tribal clan, so that every Israelite will possess the inheritance of their ancestors. 9 No inheritance may pass from one tribe to another, for each Israelite tribe is to keep the land it inherits." 10 So Zelophehad's daughters did as the Lord commanded Moses. 11 Zelophehad's daughters—Mahlah, Tirzah, Hoglah, Milkah and Noah—married their cousins on their father's side. 12 They married within the clans of the descendants of Manasseh son of Joseph, and their inheritance remained in their father's tribe and clan.– Numbers 36: 5-12 5

On one hand, females were permitted to inherit land. On the other hand, they had to marry within their tribe to protect their inheritance. On one hand, females were given power by possession until they married. On the other hand, there was inbreeding, which apparently was a lesser concern than that of keeping the land in the possession of the Manasseh tribe. One step forward for women, three steps backward toward genetic disorders.

Verse 12-13: 12 Yet the Manassites were not able to occupy these towns, for the Canaanites were determined to live in that region. 13 However, when the Israelites grew stronger, they subjected the Canaanites to forced labor but did not drive them out completely.

Forced labor for the Canaanites was discussed previously, but in these verses, it appears that it happened over a period of time until the Israelites had more strength to subject the Canaanites. After the Manassites were satisfied, Joshua received complaints from the tribe of Joseph that their land was not big enough for them and their Canaanite laborers. He gave them an option for enlarging their territory.

Verse 14-17: "If you are so numerous," Joshua answered, "and if the hill country of Ephraim is too small for you, go up into the forest and clear land for yourselves there in the land of the Perizzites and Rephaites."

Reflection:

1. How did Joshua perform as a leader in solving land disputes? Did he continue to obey God in his decision making?

2. What would be the advantages of a female landowner marrying someone in her own tribe, other than keeping possession of the land within the family?

3. What would be the disadvantages of a female landowner not marrying?

LEADERSHIP TIP #17: GREAT LEADERS CAN BE MEN OR WOMEN.

When the Lord commanded inheritance to go to each of the twelve tribes, the law was written only for males. The tribe of Manasseh had a problem: only female heirs. The daughters spoke up and asked Joshua for their inheritance, which was granted to them. Note that this tip states that great leaders CAN be women, but the Manasseh women's privilege of land ownership was neutralized once they married, and they were required to marry a relative. The women fought for their land, but apparently their women's liberation movement did not get too far..

Response:

_____

_____

_____

_____

_____

_____

_____

_____

CHAPTER EIGHTEEN

GREAT LEADERS ASK GREAT QUESTIONS, DELEGATE, AND SET EXPECTATIONS

Summary:

Verse 1: The whole assembly of the Israelites gathered at Shiloh and set up the tent of meeting there. The country was brought under their control,

Joshua and the Israelite army had made a swift conquest of the Promised Land. Then they all came together for corporate worship at the tent of meeting. This was the place where God could "tabernacle" with them. While each tribe was being allotted their land to make a life in the Promised Land, it was important to keep the focus on their one God, who had provided it all to them.

Verse 2: but there were still seven Israelite tribes who had not yet received their inheritance.

Out of the twelve tribes, only five had moved into their new homelands. The other seven still had work to do to fulfill God's promise.

Verse 3: So Joshua said to the Israelites: "How long will you wait before you begin to take possession of the land that the Lord, the God of your ancestors, has given you?

Joshua was a strong leader who had taken charge of the conquest of the Promised Land. Apparently he had been waiting on action from the seven tribes, but he continued to take charge of the process by conducting a land survey and distributing the land that had not yet been occupied by the tribes of Israel.

Verses 4-6: Appoint three men from each tribe. I will send them out to make a survey of the land and to write a description of it, according to the inheritance of each. Then they will return to me. 6 After you have written descriptions of the seven parts of the land, bring them here to me and I will cast lots for you in the presence of the Lord our God.

Verse 11: The first lot came up for the tribe of Benjamin according to its clans. Their allotted territory lay between the tribes of Judah and Joseph:

Verse 12-28: The list of the towns allotted to the tribe of Benjamin, according to its clans.

Reflection:

1. When God has called me to action, have I ever tarried to the point when he would ask me, "How long will you wait before you begin...?"

2. Is there a blessing waiting for me from God that I have delayed in taking the action needed to bring it to fulfillment? If so, what do I need to do? Who can help lead me to the appropriate strategy to make it happen?

LEADERSHIP TIP #18: GREAT LEADERS ASK GREAT QUESTIONS, DELEGATE, AND SET EXPECTATIONS.

Joshua's question to the Israelites was, "How long will you wait before you begin to take possession of the land that the Lord, the God of your ancestors, has given you?" This question is rich with nuances and opinions. Obviously, Joshua thought it had been too long. Clearly, he expected action. Firmly, he reminded them that they were delaying a gift from God, which insinuates disrespect, not only to God, but to their ancestors. Knowing that any answer was not the right answer to this question, except that they would wait no longer, Joshua facilitated the process in moving the people toward his expected results. He gave each tribe the authority to choose three men to survey the land, to write a description of it, and to return to Joshua for his assignment of land through the casting of lots in the presence of God. He included the people in part of the decision making, i.e. choosing their own surveyors, and then set the expectations and held them accountable to him for their results.

"God is still asking us, 'How long before you possess the promises I have for you?' God has many great and precious promises that we have not claimed!" — Debbie Day

Response:

CHAPTER NINETEEN

GREAT LEADERS SHOW GREAT HUMILITY

Summary:

Verse 1: The second lot came out for the tribe of Simeon according to its clans. Their inheritance lay within the territory of Judah.

Verse 10: The third lot came up for Zebulun according to its clans:

Verse 17: The fourth lot came out for Issachar according to its clans.

Verse 24: The fifth lot came out for the tribe of Asher according to its clans.

Verse 32: The sixth lot came out for Naphtali according to its clans:

Verse 40: The seventh lot came out for the tribe of Dan according to its clans.

Verses 49-50: 49 When they had finished dividing the land into its allotted portions, the Israelites gave Joshua son of Nun an inheritance among them, 50 as the Lord had commanded. They gave him the town he asked for—Timnath Serah in the hill country of Ephraim. And he built up the town and settled there.

Joshua was from the tribe of Ephraim, which had already been allotted land. After all the land had been allotted, the Israelites gave him a gift of the town of Timnath Serah as a gift and inheritance to him. The gift was not just a portion from his tribe, but a gift from the entire nation of Israel, a sign of appreciation to a leader by all of his followers. As the leader and conquest leader, he could have taken the first and the best for himself, but he did not. He did not command; the Lord commanded this gift, and he asked for a town in his tribe's allotment. Once he received the town of his choice, he made something better of it: "and he built up the town and settled there" among his tribe and his nation. After all the land was conquered and ready to be settled, Joshua continued to be the leader that God called him to be: not only strong, courageous, and noble, but also obedient and humble of heart.

Reflection:

1. What lessons do I want to take from Joshua regarding leadership?

2. What leader(s) do I know who lead like Joshua?

3. How can I grow to be stronger, more courageous, more obedient, and more humble of heart?

4. Joshua "built up" his town and settled there. How have I built up my town or the place where I live? What else could I do to be a witness for the Lord in my locale?

LEADERSHIP TIP #19: GREAT LEADERS SHOW GREAT HUMILITY.

Humbly Joshua waited until all the tribes had received their inheritance. Humbly, Joshua did not demand his inheritance, but asked his people for it. Humbly, Joshua did not choose the biggest or most important city for himself. He chose a town that needed to be "built up." Great leaders know to take care of their people first before rewarding themselves for success. Great leaders work for continuous improvement everywhere they go and everywhere they live.

"Jesus is the greatest example of a leader's humility. He was a servant who not only washed his follower's feet, but laid down His life." — Debbie Day

Response:

_____

_____

_____

CHAPTER TWENTY

GREAT LEADERS SEEK JUSTICE AND LOVE MERCY

Summary:

Verses 1-6: 1 Then the Lord said to Joshua: 2 "Tell the Israelites to designate the cities of refuge, as I instructed you through Moses, 3 so that anyone who kills a person accidentally and unintentionally may flee there and find protection from the avenger of blood. 4 When they flee to one of these cities, they are to stand in the entrance of the city gate and state their case before the elders of that city. Then the elders are to admit the fugitive into their city and provide a place to live among them. 5 If the avenger of blood comes in pursuit, the elders must not surrender the fugitive, because the fugitive killed their neighbor unintentionally and without malice aforethought. 6 They are to stay in that city until they have stood trial before the assembly and until the death of the high priest who is serving at that time. Then they may go back to their own home in the town from which they fled." so that anyone who kills a person accidentally and unintentionally may flee there and find protection from the avenger of blood.

Cities of refuge were first commanded by the Lord to Moses, and through Moses to Joshua.

Then the Lord said to Moses: 10 "Speak to the Israelites and say to them: 'When you cross the Jordan into Canaan, 11 select some towns to be your cities of refuge, to which a person who has killed someone accidentally may flee. 12 They will be places of refuge from the avenger, so that anyone accused of murder may not die before they stand trial before the assembly. 13 These six towns you give will be your cities of refuge. 14 Give three on this side of the Jordan and three in Canaan as cities of refuge. 15 These six towns will be a place of refuge for Israelites and for foreigners residing among them, so that anyone who has killed another accidentally can flee there. — Numbers 35:9-15

Consider the day in Egypt when Moses killed an Egyptian for beating a Hebrew slave. The next day when he addressed two Hebrews fighting, Moses tried to intervene, to which they asked him, "Who made you ruler and judge over us?" (Exodus 2:14) (Little did those men know that one day Moses would be ruler and judge over them.) When this news reached Pharaoh, he tried to kill Moses, but Moses fled to Midian, where he married into the family of Jethro (aka Reuel) and had children. It was while shepherding flocks near Midian that Moses met the Lord in the burning bush. In a practical sense, Midian was a "city of refuge" for Moses, even though Midian was not created for that purpose. There were no cities of refuge mentioned in the bible until the designations for the Promised Land.

In the book of Numbers, Scripture says that Moses was told by God to select towns to be designated as places of refuge for people accused of murder to wait until they could stand trial before the assembly. They would be safe from the "avengers of blood" who wanted to settle a score themselves without a judge or assembly to decide. In the book of Joshua, God repeats his commands about the cities of refuge to Joshua, "as I instructed you through Moses".

From his personal experience, Moses had a need for a place to go for refuge, and eventually met God there. Moses must have been very grateful to God for establishing a system of justice for accidental deaths (even though Moses' murder of the Egyptian was not accidental). Imagine that conversation between Moses and Joshua when they were given instructions for the cities of refuge. As old men tend to do, Moses most likely recounted his week-long trek from Egypt to Midian, where he met his future wife as he sat down to rest. The meeting at the Midian well was a watershed moment for Moses, which would be followed by his encounter with God in the burning bush, where he was called to the leadership of his people.

While taking refuge in MIdian, the leader of Israel was getting prepared by God to lead the Israelites to the Promised Land.

It would be generations later that another man would sit down to rest at a well at Sychar (aka Shechem) and ask a Samaritan woman to draw him a drink of water. This encounter would be even more spectacular than Moses' encounter with Zipporah and the other daughters of Reuel. Instead of meeting a woman to marry, Jesus met a woman and offered her "living water", and she became the first to recognize him as the Messiah and to tell others.

Verse 7: So they set apart Kedesh in Galilee in the hill country of Naphtali, Shechem in the hill country of Ephraim, and Kiriath Arba (that is, Hebron) in the hill country of Judah.

Today there are refugee camps and safe harbors for people who need to seek asylum or safety. For all of us, Psalm 46:1 says: *God is our refuge and strength, an ever-present help in trouble.*

Reflection:

1. Who or what are my places of refuge in my times of trouble?

2. Are there any times in my life when I have been close to death, but God has saved me? How did my life change after that?

3. What defining moments or places make up part of my life story, one that I retell to others about how God has saved me and has given me a new purpose?

LEADERSHIP TIP #20: GREAT LEADERS SEEK JUSTICE AND LOVE MERCY.

Joshua assigned cities of refuge for the process of justice to be carried out. Mercy was granted to people accused of murder. They could remain in a safe place until they were found innocent or guilty. Vigilantes were not permitted to take justice into their own hands. Great leaders put processes in place to protect their people from being hurt by others unjustly. This includes physical, emotional, and mental harm.

Response:

_____

_____

_____

_____

_____

_____

_____

_____

_____

_____

_____

_____

_____

_____

CHAPTER TWENTY-ONE

GREAT LEADERS
TREAT PEOPLE
EQUITABLY

Summary:

Verses 1-3: 1 Now the family heads of the Levites approached Eleazar the priest, Joshua son of Nun, and the heads of the other tribal families of Israel 2 at Shiloh in Canaan and said to them, "The Lord commanded through Moses that you give us towns to live in, with pasturelands for our livestock." 3 So, as the Lord had commanded, the Israelites gave the Levites the following towns and pasturelands out of their own inheritance: 4 The first lot came out for the Kohathites, according to their clans. The Levites who were descendants of Aaron the priest were allotted thirteen towns from the tribes of Judah, Simeon and Benjamin.

The Levites, who were set aside to tend to the tent of meeting and temple of the Lord, did not receive an inheritance of land by God as with the other eleven tribes. However, they were given towns and pasturelands for their livestock from the inheritance of the Israelites. A portion of Israel's inheritance went to their priests, the Levites. This is a model for us today, as we tithe to the church to take care of our spiritual leaders so that they can dedicate their lives to caring for the things of God, his place of worship, and the work of God.

Note that scripture says that the Levites did not come making demands of Joshua, but stated the command of God through Moses, as had been made public knowledge to all of Israel.

Verse 5: The rest of Kohath's descendants were allotted ten towns from the clans of the tribes of Ephraim, Dan and half of Manasseh.

Verse 6: The descendants of Gershon were allotted thirteen towns from the clans of the tribes of Issachar, Asher, Naphtali and the half-tribe of Manasseh in Bashan.

Verse 7: The descendants of Merari, according to their clans, received twelve towns from the tribes of Reuben, Gad and Zebulun.

Verse 8: So the Israelites allotted to the Levites these towns and their pasturelands, as the Lord had commanded through Moses.

The list of gifts from the Israelites to the Levites were allotted to each of the four Levite clans:

Kohath, Gershon, Merari, and Aaron. The list of tribes giving part of their inheritance to the Levites are listed: Judah, Simeon, Benjamin, Dan, Issachar, Asher, Naphtali, Reuben, Gad, Zebulun, and Joseph. (Joseph's house had combined tribes of Ephraim and Manasseh)

All eleven tribes gave part of their inheritance to the tribe of Levi. No one tribe covered another tribe's portion or hedged on their gift. Consider today in church budgets when the tendency is for a small minority of the congregation to cover the majority of the church expenses. If all the people gave just their 10% tithe, the church budgets could be so much more!

Verse 12: But the fields and villages around the city they had given to Caleb son of Jephunneh as his possession.

Verse 13: So to the descendants of Aaron the priest they gave Hebron (a city of refuge for one accused of murder),

Verse 43: So the Lord gave Israel all the land he had sworn to give their ancestors, and they took possession of it and settled there.

Verse 44: The Lord gave them rest on every side, just as he had sworn to their ancestors. Not one of their enemies withstood them; the Lord gave all their enemies into their hands.

Can you feel the peace covering the tribes of Israel at this time? After all the conquests and division of land, finally all had possession of a part of the Promised Land as their inheritance, and all were settled. Ahhh....but just wait; soon after the in-fighting began that almost led the people back to war again, except this time against each other. (See Chapter 22 ahead.)

Verse 45: Not one of all the Lord's good promises to Israel failed; every one was fulfilled.

Every one of God's promises was fulfilled. This verse alone is encouragement for every believer today to keep faith that God keeps his promises to us through all generations.

Reflection:

1. Do I believe that every word that God has spoken is true?

2. Do I believe that every one of God's promises will be fulfilled?

3. Am I waiting for a promise from God? Can I keep strong faith during the times when I do not see the promise being fulfilled?

4. Am I faithful to give my tithe (first fruits) to the "priests" and spiritual leaders of my church? Do I give my portion, as commanded by God through scripture? If not, what do I have to do for that to happen?

5. Do I feel rested and settled, knowing that God will provide and will fulfill his promises?

LEADERSHIP TIP #21: GREAT LEADERS TREAT PEOPLE EQUITABLY.

Since the Levites were set aside to care for the places of worship, they were not given an inheritance like the other tribes. Their "inheritance" was serving in God's temple and receiving the food from the sacrificial offerings. Under Joshua's leadership and God's commands, each tribe gave a portion of land from their own inheritance to the Levites. Everyone contributed, and as a result, the Levites received their inheritance of land. Great leaders ensure that people are treated as fairly and as equitably as possible.

Response:

_____

_____

_____

_____

_____

_____

_____

_____

_____

_____

_____

_____

_____

_____

CHAPTER TWENTY-TWO

GREAT LEADERS
KNOW HOW TO
SETTLE CONFLICTS
PEACEFULLY

Summary:

Verses 1-5: 1 Then Joshua summoned the Reubenites, the Gadites and the half-tribe of Manasseh 2 and said to them, "You have done all that Moses the servant of the Lord commanded, and you have obeyed me in everything I commanded. 3 For a long time now—to this very day—you have not deserted your fellow Israelites but have carried out the mission the Lord your God gave you. 4 Now that the Lord your God has given them rest as he promised, return to your homes in the land that Moses the servant of the Lord gave you on the other side of the Jordan. 5 But be very careful to keep the commandment and the law that Moses the servant of the Lord gave you: to love the Lord your God, to walk in obedience to him, to keep his commands, to hold fast to him and to serve him with all your heart and with all your soul."

Even though these three tribes were given land east of the Jordan River, their warriors were asked to cross over with the rest of the tribes of Israel in order to help them conquer all the land promised to Israel by God. Once their mission was accomplished, they were sent home to settle their own lands.

This short message is a powerful affirmation, confirmation, and charge by a great leader for his tribes of Reuben, Gad, and Manasseh's half tribe. The following is a list of ten paraphrased tenets from Joshua's "state of the nations" address from verses 1-5:

1. You have done all that was asked of you by God, by Moses, and by Joshua. (appreciating their obedience)

2. You have not deserted your fellow Israelites. (appreciating their loyalty)

3. You stayed faithful to the mission. (appreciating their faithfulness)

4. Return to your homes that Moses gave you on the other side of the Jordan. (confirming that their mission was completed)

5. Be very careful to keep the commandment and law of

Moses. (charging them with vigilance)

6. Love the Lord your God. (reminding them of the first commandment)

7. Walk in obedience to God. (charging them to continue their walk with God)

8. Keep God's commands. (repeating the importance of staying true to the commands)

9. Hold fast to God. (charging them to keep the faith)

10. Serve God with all your heart and with all your soul. (charging them to serve God wholeheartedly)

Verse 6: Then Joshua blessed them and sent them away, and they went to their homes.

In addition to affirming their faithfulness to Moses, to Joshua, and to God, Joshua topped off this incredible moment with his blessing.

Verse 7: (To the half-tribe of Manasseh Moses had given land in Bashan, and to the other half of the tribe Joshua gave land on the west side of the Jordan along with their fellow Israelites.) When Joshua sent them home, he blessed them,

This series of blessings was a sacred culmination of the difficult journey from captivity in Egypt to their freedom to live in their own lands.

Verse 10: When they came to Geliloth near the Jordan in the land of Canaan, the Reubenites, the Gadites and the half-tribe of Manasseh built an imposing altar there by the Jordan.

The three tribes returning to the eastern side of the Jordan stopped to build an altar, an imposing altar, which came with protests and anger from the rest of the Israelite nation.

Verse 12: the whole assembly of Israel gathered at Shiloh to go to war against them.

All the people living on the west side of the Jordan gathered with the intention to wage war against their brothers from the east side. This was shaping up to be a dramatic altercation like that of today's West Side Story! As a wise decision, they sent for a priest to ask the east siders their reason for building such an imposing altar. Were they reverting back to idol worship? The west siders demanded to know!

> *Verse 13: So the Israelites sent Phinehas son of Eleazar, the priest, to the land of Gilead—to Reuben, Gad and the half-tribe of Manasseh.*
>
> *Verse 16: "The whole assembly of the Lord says: 'How could you break faith with the God of Israel like this? How could you turn away from the Lord and build yourselves an altar in rebellion against him now?*
>
> *Verse 19: If the land you possess is defiled, come over to the Lord's land, where the Lord's tabernacle stands, and share the land with us. But do not rebel against the Lord or against us by building an altar for yourselves, other than the altar of the Lord our God.*

The people questioned the altar builders about their motivations, presuming that they broke faith with God, that they built an altar for themselves, that their land of possession was defiled in some way. The people offered a solution of sharing their land if the eastern land was defiled, a solution to use the Lord's tabernacle instead of the imposing altar. Their questions were embedded with blame and assumptions but with a need for answers, since they would not have wanted to pay the price of sin from one tribe that would possibly bring repercussions upon all of the tribes. Verse 19 says, "But do not rebel against the Lord or against us..."

> *Verse 20: When Achan son of Zerah was unfaithful in regard to the devoted things, did not wrath come on the whole community of Israel? He was not the only one who died for his sin.'"*

Included in the barrage of accusations was a warning and

reminder of what happened to Achan and family when he sinned against God. After hearing everything that the people had to say in front of the assembly and the priest, the accused tribes present their defense in the following nine verses.

Verses 21-29: Then Reuben, Gad and the half-tribe of Manasseh replied to the heads of the clans of Israel: 22 "The Mighty One, God, the Lord! The Mighty One, God, the Lord! He knows! And let Israel know! If this has been in rebellion or disobedience to the Lord, do not spare us this day. 23 If we have built our own altar to turn away from the Lord and to offer burnt offerings and grain offerings, or to sacrifice fellowship offerings on it, may the Lord himself call us to account. 24 "No! We did it for fear that some day your descendants might say to ours, 'What do you have to do with the Lord, the God of Israel? 25 The Lord has made the Jordan a boundary between us and you—you Reubenites and Gadites! You have no share in the Lord.' So your descendants might cause ours to stop fearing the Lord. 26 "That is why we said, 'Let us get ready and build an altar—but not for burnt offerings or sacrifices.' 27 On the contrary, it is to be a witness between us and you and the generations that follow, that we will worship the Lord at his sanctuary with our burnt offerings, sacrifices and fellowship offerings. Then in the future your descendants will not be able to say to ours, 'You have no share in the Lord.' 28 "And we said, 'If they ever say this to us, or to our descendants, we will answer: Look at the replica of the Lord's altar, which our ancestors built, not for burnt offerings and sacrifices, but as a witness between us and you.' 29 "Far be it from us to rebel against the Lord and turn away from him today by building an altar for burnt offerings, grain offerings and sacrifices, other than the altar of the Lord our God that stands before his tabernacle."

The defendants' first words were of praise and glory to God with the acclamation that the Lord knows the truth. Then they added a "just so you know" comment not to spare them if they were being rebellious or disobedient and acknowledging that God would be the one calling them into account. Next came a resounding NO with the explanation that they were afraid that some day the descendants of the western tribes would disown the eastern tribes because of the boundary made naturally by the Jordan River. By the eastern tribes building an imposing altar on the western shore, they would have concrete evidence that they were a part of the nation of Israel and a part of God's Promised Land. Their presence on the western shores was evidence that they fought with the rest of Israel, that they traveled the western territories in conquest for the eastern tribes, and that they did not disconnect from the Israel nation. They did not want any of their descendants to stop fearing the Lord because they were disowned by the Israel nation.

The defendants restated their faithfulness to the Lord and to their worship at the tabernacle.

There was a previous time in their history when one of their own was once in power but then discarded when a new king took the throne. Remember Joseph in Exodus 1:8?

Then a new king, to whom Joseph meant nothing, came to power in Egypt. — Exodus 1:8

A new king came to power intimidated by their numbers, then poof! The Israelites become slaves to the king. Having this quick turn of events go badly very quickly, it is plausible to think that life situations could change through the generations. Because the tribes of Reuben, Gad, and half-Manasseh settled down on the opposite side of everyone else, their geographical position could wrongly be perceived as not being a part of Israel and the nation under their one God. Hmmm...one nation under God. That has a familiar ring to it.

The "imposing altar" could be seen as an ancient way of solidifying God's promise and allocation of their Promised Land "in stone." Should there be any question of their inheritance, legacy, and membership in the nation of Israel, there was a huge pile of stones left as their "signature" on the west bank of the Jordan.

Verse 30: When Phinehas the priest and the leaders of the community—the heads of the clans of the Israelites—heard what

Reuben, Gad and Manasseh had to say, they were pleased. 31: And Phinehas son of Eleazar, the priest, said to Reuben, Gad and Manasseh, "Today we know that the Lord is with us, because you have not been unfaithful to the Lord in this matter. Now you have rescued the Israelites from the Lord's hand."

Verdict: not guilty as charged! The priest and the leaders listened to the eastsiders and believed their words of defense. The priest, Phinehas, admits that there has been a misunderstanding by confirming that they were not unfaithful and that the Israelites would not suffer any punishment from the Lord.

Verse 34: And the Reubenites and the Gadites gave the altar this name: A Witness Between Us—that the Lord is God.

As with all important milestones, the altar was given the name "Witness Between Us–that the Lord is God." Not only do I love the efforts taken to protect the integrity and faithful standing of future generations, I would also love the name of their defense attorney. Well played. Well spoken. Well done!

Reflection:

1. How important is it for accusers to wait to hear from the accused before passing judgment and blame?

2. How important is it for the accused to stay calm and listen to the accusers' entire accusation before responding?

3. What can I do to help undergird the faith of my future generations? What tangible way can I leave evidence for them to know the legacy of our family's faith?

4. How can I use this example in settling disputes among family, friends, or church members?

LEADERSHIP TIP #22: GREAT LEADERS KNOW HOW TO SETTLE CONFLICTS PEACEFULLY.

Misunderstandings and assumptions can lead quickly to violence if leaders do not intervene. Wisely the Israelites sent for Phineas, the priest, to help settle the dispute. The west side tribes thought that the east siders were building an altar for themselves. Behind the kerfuffle was the insecurity of the east side tribes, who were afraid that their future generations might be disowned or disconnected from the rest of the nation of Israel. After all perspectives were shared, both sides understood each other, and peace ensued. Great leaders are called upon for solutions when trouble arises. Great leaders seek peaceful solutions, which require attentive listening, patience, and seeking the truth.

Response:

_____

_____

_____

_____

_____

_____

_____

_____

CHAPTER TWENTY-THREE

GREAT LEADERS LEAVE A LEGACY OF WISDOM

Summary:

Verses 1-5: After a long time had passed and the Lord had given Israel rest from all their enemies around them, Joshua, by then a very old man, 2 summoned all Israel—their elders, leaders, judges and officials—and said to them: "I am very old. 3 You yourselves have seen everything the Lord your God has done to all these nations for your sake; it was the Lord your God who fought for you. 4 Remember how I have allotted as an inheritance for your tribes all the land of the nations that remain—the nations I conquered— between the Jordan and the Mediterranean Sea in the west. 5 The Lord your God himself will push them out for your sake. He will drive them out before you, and you will take possession of their land, as the Lord your God promised you.

Joshua communicated consistently with his people about their relationship with God and each other. Admittedly, Joshua and his commanders had not eradicated the previous inhabitants entirely, and this must have been on his mind as he came closer to death. He conceded that he is a very old man, and as very old people want to do, Joshua shared his best wisdom and warnings with his people on a matter that was on his heart. In order for future generations to stay faithful to God and to obey all the Law of Moses, they were not to associate with the survivors of the conquests. If they did decide to intermarry and associate with them and serve other gods, all that Israel had fought for would perish. The Lord's anger would burn, and all would be lost–quickly. Imagine hearing the following words from a great leader who had grown very old, speaking with the voice of wisdom and a tone of warning.

Verse 6: "Be very strong; be careful to obey all that is written in the Book of the Law of Moses, without turning aside to the right or to the left.

Verse 7: Do not associate with these nations that remain among you; do not invoke the names of their gods or swear by them. You must not serve them or bow down to them.

How much of our modern culture seeps into our lives through casual meaningless expressions, like "Oh, my god!" or "I swear to God...!" How many homes have Ouija boards as party games for children? One could look closer at city buildings shaped like pyramids or Renaissance Festivals selling items of the occult to see how much we are pulled away from holiness and purity of living. Some folks would argue how ridiculous and harmless all of this is to our faith, but there are many warnings from very wise old men, like Joshua, not to be turned to the right or to the left.

Verse 8: But you are to hold fast to the Lord your God, as you have until now.

Verse 11: So be very careful to love the Lord your God.

Verse 12: "But if you turn away and ally yourselves with the survivors of these nations that remain among you and if you intermarry with them and associate with them,

Verse 16: If you violate the covenant of the Lord your God, which he commanded you, and go and serve other gods and bow down to them, the Lord's anger will burn against you, and you will quickly perish from the good land he has given you."

This verse is a good example of the "fear of the Lord" in a way that acknowledges God's awesome power over life and death. Joshua had to have known that another leader would be soon called by God to take his place. Would it be a stronger leader who would keep the people on track? Or would it be a weaker leader who would lose all the good land that God had given them. Not knowing the future, Joshua used his final words to emphasize the Lord's covenant in front of all the elders, leaders, judges, and officials of Israel.

Reflection:

1. How much wisdom can I learn from Joshua's words to his community of believers?

2. What can I do or say to younger leaders and the next generation to guide them to hold fast to the Lord and to be careful to love the Lord?

3. Is it possible to intermarry with non-believers and not be influenced by their different beliefs and way of life? How would I go about supporting believers in an interfaith marriage?

4. How do I define and describe the "fear of the Lord" in my life? Afraid of God? In awe of God? Reverent? Is fear of the Lord different or the same in the Old Testament under the Law of Moses and the New Testament under the New Covenant of Jesus Christ's death and resurrection?

LEADERSHIP TIP #23: GREAT LEADERS LEAVE A LEGACY OF WISDOM.

Joshua shared the importance of following God's law and refraining from associating with foreigners with foreign gods. He placed special emphasis on the consequences of disobedience: death and the loss of their precious land that they had worked so hard to inherit. Great leaders share their wisdom with their people, not only for encouragement and life lessons, but for living their best lives.

Response:

_____

_____

CHAPTER TWENTY-FOUR

GREAT LEADERS INSPIRE

Summary:

Verse 1: Then Joshua assembled all the tribes of Israel at Shechem. He summoned the elders, leaders, judges and officials of Israel, and they presented themselves before God.

Shechem was a city of refuge that belonged to Ephraim, the tribe of Joshua. In his very old age, Joshua calls everyone to a city of refuge, typically reserved for accused murderers before they face judgment. When they gather, they present themselves before God. Perhaps Joshua was reminding everyone that all need to take refuge in God, for all fall short of God's glory.

This is a scene that recalls to mind Paul's verse in the New Testament, "All have sinned and fallen short of the glory of God" (Romans 3:23)

Compare Joshua's last words of wisdom with Moses' last words:

Assemble the people—men, women and children, and the foreigners residing in your towns—so they can listen and learn to fear the Lord your God and follow carefully all the words of this law. 13 Their children, who do not know this law, must hear it and learn to fear the Lord your God as long as you live in the land you are crossing the Jordan to possess." — Deuteronomy 31:12-13

Assemble before me all the elders of your tribes and all your officials, so that I can speak these words in their hearing and call the heavens and the earth to testify against them. 29 For I know that after my death you are sure to become utterly corrupt and to turn from the way I have commanded you. In days to come, disaster will fall on you because you will do evil in the sight of the Lord and arouse his anger by what your hands have made." —Deuteronomy 31: 28

Verse 2: Joshua said to all the people, "This is what the Lord, the God of Israel, says: 'Long ago your ancestors, including Terah the father of Abraham and Nahor, lived beyond the Euphrates River and worshiped other gods.

Verse 4: and to Isaac I gave Jacob and Esau. I assigned the hill country of Seir to Esau, but Jacob and his family went down to Egypt.

Verse 5: "'Then I sent Moses and Aaron, and I afflicted the Egyptians by what I did there, and I brought you out.

Verse 7: But they cried to the Lord for help, and he put darkness between you and the Egyptians; he brought the sea over them and covered them. You saw with your own eyes what I did to the Egyptians. Then you lived in the wilderness for a long time.

Verse 12: I sent the hornet ahead of you, which drove them out before you—also the two Amorite kings. You did not do it with your own sword and bow.

There are various interpretations of what God meant by the hornet, but the word choice evokes fear, pain, repeated attacks, and determination to harm. God took responsibility and credit for driving out the people's enemies. Message received. Ouch!

Verse 13: So I gave you a land on which you did not toil and cities you did not build; and you live in them and eat from vineyards and olive groves that you did not plant.'

This was a powerful reminder that God provided everything for them, and what he wanted in return was their faithfulness and undivided loyalty.

Verse 14: "Now fear the Lord and serve him with all faithfulness. Throw away the gods your ancestors worshiped beyond the Euphrates River and in Egypt, and serve the Lord.

Since the gods were handmade idols and inanimate objects, they really could throw their ancestral gods away–literally–and spiritually as well.

> Verse 15: But if serving the Lord seems undesirable to you, then choose for yourselves this day whom you will serve, whether the gods your ancestors served beyond the Euphrates, or the gods of the Amorites, in whose land you are living. But as for me and my household, we will serve the Lord."

This address by Joshua is powerfully reminiscent of Moses' farewell recorded in Deuteronomy.

> See, I set before you today life and prosperity, death and destruction. 16 For I command you today to love the Lord your God, to walk in obedience to him, and to keep his commands, decrees and laws; then you will live and increase, and the Lord your God will bless you in the land you are entering to possess. 17 But if your heart turns away and you are not obedient, and if you are drawn away to bow down to other gods and worship them, 18 I declare to you this day that you will certainly be destroyed. You will not live long in the land you are crossing the Jordan to enter and possess. 19 This day I call the heavens and the earth as witnesses against you that I have set before you life and death, blessings and curses. Now choose life, so that you and your children may live 20 and that you may love the Lord your God, listen to his voice, and hold fast to him. For the Lord is your life, and he will give you many years in the land he swore to give to your fathers, Abraham, Isaac and Jacob. – Deuteronomy 30: 15-20 15

After the Israelites were reminded of all the blessings from God, from their beginnings at the Euphrates River to the Promised Land, Joshua tells the people to choose for themselves whom they would serve. Moses puts the choice before the people in terms of life and death, blessings and curses. God had given them commandments and instructions, but his laws were only applied to his people, those who believed and served him. Then Joshua followed up with an emphatic statement about his choice for himself and his household: they would serve the Lord.

Today in our culture, many times free will, freedom, and free choice are used as mantras for self-satisfying decisions that fulfill human desires, not the desire to love and serve God only. When believers feel challenged by so many distractions and challenges to conform to the world, they need only remember Joshua's claim for himself and his family: "As for me and my household, we will serve the Lord."

Verse 16: Then the people answered, "Far be it from us to forsake the Lord to serve other gods!

Verse 19: Joshua said to the people, "You are not able to serve the Lord. He is a holy God; he is a jealous God. He will not forgive your rebellion and your sins.

Verse 21: But the people said to Joshua, "No! We will serve the Lord."

Verse 22: Then Joshua said, "You are witnesses against yourselves that you have chosen to serve the Lord." "Yes, we are witnesses," they replied.

Verse 23: "Now then," said Joshua, "throw away the foreign gods that are among you and yield your hearts to the Lord, the God of Israel."

Verse 24: And the people said to Joshua, "We will serve the Lord our God and obey him."

This exchange between Joshua and his people must have sounded like a pep rally of faith, or at least a dramatic corporate altar call. Emphatically, three times they promise to serve the Lord. Joshua also tells them to discard anything not of God and yield their hearts to the Lord, the God of Israel. Joshua also made a special point of calling witnesses to their vows of faithfulness to God, and all the people claim to be witnesses–for themselves individually and for others corporately.

Verse 25: On that day Joshua made a covenant for the people, and there at Shechem he reaffirmed for them decrees and laws.

In this assembly, Joshua gave the history of the covenant with God and Israel, the terms of agreement–that of choice to love and serve God, an option to serve whomever they chose; he accepted the people's vows of faithfulness three times; he renewed the covenant with God on behalf of his people; and once again, Joshua reaffirmed the decrees and laws for all the people.

Verse 26: And Joshua recorded these things in the Book of the Law of God. Then he took a large stone and set it up there under the oak near the holy place of the Lord.

Wisely, Joshua wrote the history of the renewal of the covenant in the Book of the Law of God, lest they might forget. Additionally, he gave them a large reminder of their vow to serve God in the form of a stone under a tree near the holy place–a dramatic and effective strategy.

Verse 27: "See!" he said to all the people. "This stone will be a witness against us. It has heard all the words the Lord has said to us. It will be a witness against you if you are untrue to your God."

Just in case all the witnesses flaked out on the covenant, Joshua called a witness from nature into accountability: a stone. This is the same strategy that the tribes of Reuben, Gad, and half-Manasseh used when they wanted to ensure that there was some witness to their faithfulness. Twice, stones served as witnesses in the Promised Land for future generations.

This verse is a personification of the stone hearing the words of the Lord and being a witness to speak against those who are untrue to God. In the New Testament in the Gospel of Luke, the crowd of Jesus' disciples were praising God and shouting blessings over the king coming in the name of the Lord. When the Pharisaic Jews demanded that Jesus rebuke them, Jesus replied that if they kept quiet, the stones would cry out.

When he came near the place where the road goes down the Mount of Olives, the whole crowd of disciples began joyfully to praise God in loud voices for all the miracles they had seen: 38 "Blessed is the king who comes in the name of the Lord!" "Peace in heaven and glory in the highest!" 39 Some of the Pharisees in the crowd said to Jesus, "Teacher, rebuke your disciples!" 40 "I tell you," he replied, "if they keep quiet, the stones will cry out."
— Luke 19: 38-40

When Jesus voiced his words to the Pharisees, both he and the Jewish leaders would have known the history of Joshua's stone under the oak tree near the holy place of the Lord.

References to rocks and stones serve many purposes in the Bible: memorials, altars, barriers to keep enemy kings in caves, closures for graves, witnesses to God's word, witness to the coming of the Messiah, witnesses to an empty tomb.

Hannah's prayer in 1 Samuel 2:2 refers to God as a rock:

There is no one holy like the Lord;
there is no one besides you;
there is no Rock like our God.

In Genesis 49:24 Jacob refers to God as the Rock of Israel.

Verse 28: Then Joshua dismissed the people, each to their own inheritance.

Verse 29: After these things, Joshua son of Nun, the servant of the Lord, died at the age of a hundred and ten.

Verse 31: Israel served the Lord throughout the lifetime of Joshua and of the elders who outlived him and who had experienced everything the Lord had done for Israel.

Verse 32: And Joseph's bones, which the Israelites had brought up from Egypt, were buried at Shechem in the tract of land that Jacob bought for a hundred pieces of silver from the sons of Hamor, the father of Shechem. This became the inheritance of Joseph's descendants.

Shechem, the refuge city and location of the renewed covenant, was also the place chosen to bury Joseph's bones.

Verse 33: And Eleazar son of Aaron died and was buried at Gibeah, which had been allotted to his son Phinehas in the hill country of Ephraim.

Reflection:

1. God used darkness between the Israelites and the Egyptians to protect them. Darkness is usually associated with evil or a negative state, but when has darkness been a blessing to me?

2. What blessings has God given to me that I did not ask for, work for, or expect? How did I receive them or use them to glorify God?

3. What old ancestral bad habits, cycles, sins, tendencies, etc. do I need to "put away forever"?

4. Have I chosen to serve the Lord in all ways? If I have ever chosen not to serve, then whom was I serving through that decision?

5. What idol do I need to destroy in my life?

6. Joshua declared that the huge stone had heard everything the Lord had said to them and placed it under the terebinth tree as a witness to testify against people who go back on their word to God. What tangible, visible symbol can I use to remind me never to go back on my word to God or on God's Word?

7. The bones of Joseph were buried at Shechem on the land of his descendants, the tribe of Ephraim, as were the bones of the priest Eleazar, son of Aaron. What monuments or burial grounds are sacred to me? my family? my faith? What thoughts come to my mind when I think about my death and burial?

8. What have I learned from Joshua's last words and actions that are relevant to me today?

9. Leadership challenge: after reviewing Joshua's and Moses' addresses to the people before they died, compose your last words of wisdom that you want your next generations to hear.

LEADERSHIP TIP #24: GREAT LEADERS INSPIRE.

Joshua inspired his people to serve God throughout his lifetime and beyond. He recounted their history to the point of his impending demise; he asked for their commitment to God; he recorded it in a book; and he made a tangible symbol of their commitment for them to remember long after he died. Joshua was the ultimate example of an inspiring leader. Even after he died, the people continued to serve God all throughout the lifetime of the elders who outlived him.

Verse 31: Israel served the Lord throughout the lifetime of Joshua and of the elders who outlived him and who had experienced everything the Lord had done for Israel.

Not only do great leaders inspire, but great leaders are inspired - by other people, by nature, and by God. Joshua was inspired by Moses and his predecessors. Joshua was inspired by nature as he scouted the Promised Land and saw the riches of his people's future inheritances. Joshua was inspired by God, who guided him across the Jordan River and gave him victory to occupy cities and territories in the most unusual ways.

When **people** inspire leaders, the leaders relate to some words of wisdom, actions, or ways of living that cause them to accept, adapt, and transform how they live and lead. When **nature** inspires leaders, their visceral experiences transform their attitudes, thoughts, and ways of living and leading. When **God** inspires leaders, he fulfills his purposes intended for them and for his people. Here are some ways that God inspires people to great leadership:

1. God communicates with great leaders through the Holy

Spirit, prayer, worship, the Word, signs, nature, miracles, angels, messengers, and innumerable ways that are specific for each person to understand.

2. God calls great leaders to specific roles and missions, both short and long term.

3. God ordains great leaders with the authority to lead.

4. God equips and empowers great leaders to do great things.

5. God teaches and transforms great leaders through their growth in his truth, his wisdom, courage, humility, and experiences of both successes and failures.

6. God maintains a close relationship with great leaders.

7. God never changes. His expectations are always clear and consistent.

Response:

_____

_____

_____

_____

_____

_____

_____

AFTERWORD

Afterword

If ever there were a season in society's existence as well as ministry in the church, that good leadership is essential, it is now. Much has been written about organizational and particularly ministerial leadership that so often focuses attention on the technical-rational elements of institutional management. Javelin Over Jericho dares to offer manifold differences between the pragmatism of management and the poignant promises of leadership. Additionally, Javelin Over Jericho grounds the tenets of leadership offered in this text deeply in the Word of God.

It is especially in these post-pandemic times that ministerial leadership is facing a host of challenges. Almost every church and ministry has had to deal with critical changes to how they have operated in the past. Leadership structures have been modified to adapt to the myriad nuances of ministry that have had intense impact over the last four years. And all have not made these changes grounded in a solid biblical foundation. Almost everything that could be shaken has been and only what the Lord has established remains. Javelin Over Jericho offers leaders, however, a biblical blueprint upon which to build ministerial leadership that will support leaders as they engage in these essential transitions. Leadership methods may change, but the message remains the same, and Javelin Over Jericho ably provides the substance of the permanent message.

It is very difficult to provide counterarguments to the ideas and philosophical positions Dr. Nancy Hulshult delivers in this text. Each chapter offers insights and paradigms for leaders to enhance their professional practices. Additionally, the leadership tips, such as, great leaders plan strategies, great leaders trust and are trustworthy, and great leaders adapt their strategy for their purpose, provide tremendous fodder for leaders, particularly those in ministry, to consider their leadership performance more carefully.

Javelin Over Jericho does not release the reader to merely be enamored with technique and leave abandoned the essential element of reflection that so often receives short shrift in a leader's portfolio of responsibilities. In various sections of the work devoted to reflection, questions such as who have been my mentor leaders that have encouraged or motivated me when I need it most, or what do I need to do to follow God "wholeheartedly" like Caleb, requires the reader to deal with the weightier matters of leading God's people.

So many believe they know the components of the multiple facets of leadership. They are so convinced because they would assert that they have been the followers of a host of leaders, especially leaders in ministry. However, Javelin Over Jericho enters the depths of a leader's inner space and provides answers to explain leadership behavior. It is impossible to simply read this text without becoming personally engaged. At the conclusion of each chapter, the reader is compelled to deal with their personal position on what is presented as they must belabor their journey through the twenty-four chapters by opportunities for required reflection. These are necessary blockages to reading Javelin Over Jericho without engaging in the work personally.

This work should be read multiple times to ensure a genuine grasp of the substance of the text. Indeed, Javelin Over Jericho points a positive direction for the future of ministerial leadership that sometimes suffers from the agony of misunderstanding and the proclivity to pursue the road of least resistance. Each chapter helps to do the work of leading God's people with his assurance of guidance, strength, and his powerful presence.

Michael E. Dantley, Ed. D.
Bishop and Senior Pastor
Christ Emmanuel Christian Fellowship
Cincinnati, Ohio

www.ingramcontent.com/pod-product-compliance
Lightning Source LLC
Chambersburg PA
CBHW060039150626
46553CB00017BA/592